much love
+
joy
in the
kitchen!

♡

Linda Dalal Sawaya

The Ganamey ❤ Sawaya Family Cookbook

ALICE'S KITCHEN

MY GRANDMOTHER DALAL & MOTHER ALICE'S TRADITIONAL LEBANESE COOKING

◆

Linda Dalal Sawaya

◆

RECIPES OF DALAL HAGE GANAMEY
ALICE GANAMEY SAWAYA
ELIAS GEORGE SAWAYA & LINDA DALAL SAWAYA
AS RECORDED AND INTERPRETED
BY
LINDA DALAL SAWAYA

The Ganamey ♥ Sawaya Lebanese Family Cookbook

ALICE'S KITCHEN

MY GRANDMOTHER DALAL & MOTHER ALICE'S TRADITIONAL LEBANESE COOKING

3rd edition 1997, published by Linda Sawaya Design ◆ Portland, Oregon
Text, Illustrations, Photographs copyright © 1997 Linda Dalal Sawaya
Cover design and illustration copyright © 1997 Linda Dalal Sawaya

Writing, editing, typesetting, illustration, food styling and photography, recipe testing,
book design and production by Linda Dalal Sawaya
Recipes, food styling, editing and overall assistance, love and support by Alice Ganamey Sawaya

Excerpts from the first edition appeared in *Aramco World* Magazine, January/February 1997

ISBN 0-9660492-1-7
Library of Congress Catalog Card Number 97-97027

A PORTION OF THE PROCEEDS FROM SALES OF **ALICE'S KITCHEN** WILL BENEFIT THE
PEOPLE OF LEBANON. FOR INFORMATION, ADDITIONAL BOOKS, OR COMMENTS:

Linda Sawaya Design
P. O. Box 150878
San Rafael, CA 94915

sawaya@teleport.com
http://www.teleport.com/~sawaya

ALICE'S KITCHEN

◆

*To my mother, Alice
and her mother, Dalal
and her mother, Sharife
and to all the mothers before them
and to all the children after them*

and

*To my father, Elias,
whose tomato salad was made with love.*

*In commemoration of
the hundredth anniversary of his birth.
1895-1995*

And to Lebanon, our mother land, to heal.

❤

ALICE'S KITCHEN

ABOUT THIS EDITION

More than twenty years ago, the idea to record our family recipes for a cookbook enthusiastically began and took root—my epicurean Mama, Alice, created beautiful food, I photographed it, recorded recipes on index cards and then moved to Portland. Countless long distance calls asking, "Mom, how do you make....?" transpired over the years. Her responses were scribbled on anything handy; the food cooked and enjoyed. The box full of handwritten notes on index cards was typed into my computer in 1990. A year later, the smeared recipes on snipets of paper were typed in: editing continued; self-imposed deadlines came and went.

Finally, in December 1992, a few copies of the first edition, essentially a tiny draft, were printed and shared with my family and friends for Christmas; a few were sold to help cover printing costs. More recipe gathering, testing, questions to Mother, more stories shared, recipes clarified, and inconsistencies eliminated, such as the ten different ways I spelled *hommous* or *m'jaddrah*. These transliterated Arabic words appear in *italics* and are my interpretation of our family's pronunciation of them.

In 1994, *Aramco World* magazine asked about publishing an excerpt from my little book. In January/February 1997, Alice and I became *Aramco World* cover girls!—and, along with eight pages in the magazine from **Alice's Kitchen**, we went all over the world. My gratitude to them for their fine publication and excellent editorial guidance. This launched the 2nd edition of the cookbook, which sold out quickly. Amazing letters and postcards, came from many people sharing their own family stories, bringing tears to our eyes, joy to our hearts.

No words can express my unending gratitude to my Mother, Alice, without whom this book would never be and to my family whose photos are included. This 3rd edition, the latest incarnation of the book, Fall 1997, is slightly revised, corrected and improved, the next step toward my vision of the book to be published with color illustrations, photos, and Arabic calligraphy. *Inshallah!* Your comments and feedback in response to **Alice's Kitchen** are welcomed. My sincerest appreciation to my friends Lee Ann Ward for her diligent proofreading and editing, and Josephine Raad Chism for her gracious attempts to improve my Arabic transliteration!

Welcome to **Alice's Kitchen**! *Ahlan wa Sahlan* and *Sahteyn!*

ALICE'S KITCHEN

TABLE OF CONTENTS

ALICE'S KITCHEN

INTRODUCTION

Many, many generations ago mothers began passing on to daughters the ways of preparing wonderful food that have made the Lebanese famous throughout the world. Each generation made improvements and additions to the traditions, creating a marvelous, diverse cuisine. There are mountain traditions, coastal traditions, village traditions, urban, religious and seasonal traditions. Within each of these, variations occur from place to place and family to family.

In the late 1800s when my grandmother, Dalal Hage Ganamey, whom we always called *Sitto*, was sent as a child to the convent school in her Lebanese mountain village of Douma, she was taken not into the classroom but instead, into the kitchen to cook. As a result, she didn't learn to read or write—instead, she became an incredible cook.

Alice, my mother, learned the ways of her mother, Dalal, first in Douma and then in Detroit, where the family immigrated in 1926. In 1934, Mother married my father Elias, who was living in California, thus continuing her westward migration.

Five years later, *Sitto* and *Jiddo*, my grandfather, joined them in Los Angeles. By the time I was a child, Mother and *Sitto* had become renowned for their great cooking. And I had the great fortune, as the youngest of five daughters, of being their assistant. Thus began my apprenticeship in our Lebanese kitchen. My primary role as dish-dryer and table-setter expanded after I begged to roll *waraq 'inab* and *malfouf*, stuff *kousa*, and pinch *mamools*. Most of all, I longed to twirl the bread dough high in the air and toss it from arm to arm like Mother did. Despite my pleading, handling those huge rounds

of dough was *not* a possibility. Mama refused to risk its inevitable fall to the floor from the arms of her ten year old.

Despite this setback, years later I decided to teach myself. At last, I have mastered a much smaller loaf of bread than the mammoth twenty-inch rounds that Mother twirled so effortlessly. Tiny, eight-inch rounds nevertheless thrill me as I spin them into the air—they store easily in the freezer and are quickly reheated—enriching our meals with hot bread and great memories. The stacks of fresh *khoobz marouq* wrapped in slightly dampened towels, steaming from Mama's oven, and the incomparable smell of bread as it bakes, go straight to the essence of my being. A dab of butter and a drizzle of honey on bread hot from the oven is like paradise. This is why I, too, must bake bread.

In our house there was always an abundance of food. There had to be enough: for our large family and for visitors, who were always welcomed at our table. At dinner, seconds were essential. If you refused, even after the customary three-times offering, Mother still slipped another helping onto your plate. It wasn't because she didn't want leftovers—we *loved* leftovers—it was because of *Sitto's* and Mother's tradition of generosity and their genuine desire to satisfy everyone. Sharing food was the greatest gift one could give.

Over the years our family ate traditional Lebanese mountain village cuisine modified by Mother and *Sitto* according to what was available in Los Angeles grocery and import stores in the 1950s. Whole lambs were not found in supermarkets. Mother and *Sitto* painstakingly cut legs of lamb into appropriate components for various dishes, carefully removing all but the correct bit of fat. In Douma, this had been done by the town butcher.

There, in the old country of the early 1900s, *Sitto* didn't bake her own bread; she didn't have an oven—no one but the village baker did. Her own kneaded bread dough was carried to the baker, *khoobbazze*, Aunt Adele's mother, *Sitt* Nazira Tannous Abi Samrah, to form and bake the loaves in a wood-fired oven, the *tannour*. The traditional payment for *Sitt* Nazira was a portion of the baked bread. After Mother married, she was determined to learn the difficult tech-

nique of making those huge, paper thin loaves for our family, for there was no village baker in Los Angeles.

The adaptations that Mother and *Sitto* made for the western world made sense. Our stove in Los Angeles had four burners and two ovens, instead of the typical single-burner charcoal stoves or open fires, *baroun*, of the village that led to a whole tradition of one-pot meals in early Lebanon. Certain spices and herbs were impossible to come by. Friends shared with friends the precious contents of a parcel from the old country containing *zaa'tar* or *mahlab* or special vegetable seeds to plant from the village.

We kept a small kitchen garden in our sunny California backyard, and dared to raise chickens for a while until loud phone calls from our otherwise quiet, affluent neighborhors came in, complaining of the rooster's early morning serenades. *Ba'doonis, na'na, baqleh, kousa abiad,* and *waraq 'inab, limon, akkidinne,* and *teen* graced our table with seasonal harvests that were essential to our meals, many of which were unknown and otherwise unavailable here. Having a garden and eating foods in season is our inherited ancestral tradition of living gently on the earth; using its resources respectfully; and preparing and sharing food with love.

I remember one difficulty growing up Lebanese in the 1950s in Los Angeles—going to school and taking *hommous, m'jaddrah,* or *laban* for lunch was just too strange. My sister Vivian and I, after endless teasing, begged Mother to buy bologna, American cheese, or peanut butter and jelly for sandwiches. Only at home did we devour *hommous* and everything Lebanese. Occasionally we asked Mother

to cook hamburgers or spaghetti for dinner and although she accommodated us, somehow even these ended up with parsley in them.

When I came home from school one day, I discovered *Sitto* chasing one of our chickens around the back-

yard. I was not prepared for what my eyes were about to see. Wielding a knife, she managed to capture and actually chop the head off of the poor creature, who, for what seemed like a very long time, continued running around in circles without his head. Sure enough, stuffed chicken was the special dinner that night. And, as sure as that chicken ran in circles without his head, I could not eat it.

Food, of course, is a central part of Lebanese culture. Our family dinners were a gathering time; everyone was present, we rarely ate dinner at friend's houses. More often than not, we brought school friends or neighbors home to eat our "strange" but delicious food. To us, their food was just as unfamiliar. At the dinner table, my father was overwhelmed by the energy of five daughters, but despite his longing for a son, he radiated happiness in our midst.

I remember rich moments in the kitchen after school with Mother and *Sitto*. Because Lebanese food is labor intensive, sometimes they began preparing dinner right after breakfast. When we came home from school, they were *still* cooking, and I was allowed to roll, wrap, stuff or pinch whatever was in progress. Sometimes meal preparation began days ahead: cutting the leg of lamb so that just the right bit of fat was included; making cheese; curing olives or stirring kettles of preserves to be stored for use in the days or weeks to come. Bread baking was a festive occasion in my eyes, watching mom toss the dough into the air and gracefully twirl it over her arms. Eventually, Mother let me slide the loaves off huge wooden boards that she had specially made, into our old gas Wedgewood stove in the basement. Dad had his specialties in the kitchen: his fabulous tomato salad, *laban*, and "maple syrup". Often he would come home with lugs of California fruits or huge bags of French rolls fresh from a bakery. Over the years he planted ten fig trees alongside the grapevines in our garden and tended them as Mother tended her five daughters.

MY FIRST TRIP TO LEBANON

In 1971, a three month visit to Lebanon transformed my life. It also provided the beginning of this cookbook, perhaps as much as my ancestry, my childhood and every evening meal were also the be-

ginning. The trip catalyzed my identity with my roots and showed me the fragility of our culture once transplanted to another continent. Many Lebanese-Americans in the process of assimilating into American culture often lost connection with Middle Eastern culture. Being in Lebanon delineated my duality as both an American and a Lebanese Arab, and not merely one or the other.

Flying into Beirut, I felt like I was coming home. The land of Lebanon looked so much like the southern California landscape at that time, and even more, the experience of being surrounded by an entire country of people who looked like me, spoke our language, and ate our foods, was transformative. For once, I belonged. In Lebanon, the cultural source of my family's generosity and hospitality reiterated itself in every encounter, in every greeting kissed on both cheeks, in every invitation to *ghadda*. This generosity has been an integral part of Middle Eastern life as long as memory.

The roots of Mother's artistry were visible on every dish, garnished and embellished with sprigs of parsley or mint, pine nuts, pomegranate seeds or paprika. In presentation, I saw an art form; in sharing, a ritual of pleasure and friendship. Food brings together family, friends and strangers; it is a medium for laughter and stories. It is no less powerful outside the home, where street markets, vendors, cafés and restaurants all celebrate life. When I walked Beirut's streets, saw Lebanon's orchards and delighted in its food and language, recognized its music and dance from our *mahrajans*, I felt that I had come home. Lebanon in 1971 was lovely.

Lovely, and yet, this paradise found of Lebanon was mortally fragile. No one could have believed that a war was imminent that was to last almost twenty years and irrevocably transform Lebanon. If one did not pay attention to the many Palestinian refugees camped in the empty lots and open spaces of Beirut and its suburbs, it was a heavenly place.

I saw refugees camped throughout Beirut and in the countryside, along the *snobar* lined road from the airport, that the Israelis later bombed and burned all the way to the Burj and the port. Refugees were camped under trees that would be the pride of any urban

capital and in cardboard shelters where there were no trees. It was wintertime in Beirut, and the pressure of 100,000 refugees built up over many years, stressed the people and their infrastructure to a breaking point. I felt the tension building, but no one including myself could foresee the depth and scope of the tragedy yet to come to this incredibly lovely land—a land whose peoples were to be shattered and scattered for years. Greed and denial, war and divisiveness, occupation and repression, daily tragedy and violence visited a land where ease, generosity and hospitality had been an integral part of community life for centuries.

At that time, for me to be traveling alone to Lebanon was disconcerting for my relatives since women, young or old, did not typically travel alone. In those days, even going alone to downtown Beirut was unthinkable for some Lebanese women. What I was doing was considered outrageous to my relatives; yet they comforted themselves in the thought that I was sent there to find a husband, until I told them that was not why I was there. In disbelief, they nevertheless introduced me to what seemed to be *every* available young man in Lebanon. Oh how American I felt then! Indeed, I was young, a first generation American, a feminist and a Lebanese. I returned to the states transformed with greater awareness and intrigue of my cultural heritage and of the political crisis that was unfolding.

And as much as I felt I had found home in Lebanon, I also found how American I am. My journey congealed the mix of values within me that is a combination of old and new, Middle Eastern and western, Lebanese and American, manifested in my life through cooking, art and gardening. And Lebanon was a sensory feast—of the visual, auditory, and culinary realms.

One of the most wonderful meals I remember was at an outdoor restaurant in Chtoura, a little town overlooking the Bekaa Valley on the way to the ruins at Baalbaak. We ate *mezza* consisting of at least fifty tiny oval plates filled with delicacies from small grilled birds to *fistook*, and Lebanese classics from *hommous* and *baba ghannouj* to *tabbouli*. We sat in the sunshine gazing at the expansive, tranquil farmland that provided this abundance. From that moment I understood that *mezza* is the heart of Lebanese cuisine, just as

lamb and rice are its backbone, *laban*, olives and bread its fragrant spirit, garlic and onions its soul, and mint and salads its breath.

The food of Lebanon evolved over the centuries: a little meat and lots of fresh vegetables, grains, herbs and seasonings aromatically combined. Many Lebanese dishes provide complementary proteins, that is, complete protein formed by combining two non-meat foods, such as legumes with grains, or seeds and nuts with grains. Lentils and rice in the one-pot dish, *m'jaddrah*, are one example; *hommous b'tahini*, puréed garbanzo beans with a sauce made from ground sesame seeds, eaten with wheat bread, is another. Complementary proteins evolved as a major part of the diet where Christian practices such as Lent, *siyem*, economic circumstances, and the scarcity of meat create a need for meatless protein sources.

Traditional Lebanese cuisine uses relatively small amounts of meat, almost always lamb. When meat is eaten, every part of the lamb is utilized, even the head, and none of the lamb is wasted—there are recipes which use virtually every part of the animal. On my trip to Lebanon I ate wonderful little omelettes—until I found out that they were filled with *cerveau*, brains. I also ate a bite of a *baydaat ghanem* sandwich—lamb's testicle—of course without knowing what it was until too late. My squeamishness was the only problem and both were difficult to swallow once I found out what I was eating. At home, my sisters and I refused to even taste *ghamme*, tripe, or tongue, *l'senn*, while Mother, Dad, *Sitto* and Uncle Edmond relished them as the delicacies they were.

Poor people have traditionally had less access to meat. In our village when my parents were growing up, chicken dinner was the Sunday feast. In America, beef production (and perhaps lamb) is accomplished by means of excessive use of grains which are suitable themselves for consumption (see Francis Moore Lappé's book, *Diet for a Small Planet*). Methane produced by cattle is said to be seriously harming the ozone layer. In Lebanon sheep are strictly grazing animals and do not eat grain that humans could eat. These facts make the Lebanese diet both less expensive and more healthful than diets heavy on beef. A few cubes of lamb on a *shish kabob* is typically the most meat an average person would eat. Lamb com-

bines with bulgar in some recipes, successfully extending the quantity, adding flavor, protein and other nutrition.

Lebanese food, a model of the healthy Mediterranean diet, is fast being integrated into the American diet, just as pizza, stir-fried dishes, tacos, and crepes have been in the past. *Tabbouli, hommous,* and *falafel* appear regularly in newspaper recipe columns and they are available in health food stores, supermarkets and delis. Pocket bread is in vogue. And with olive oil as its main fat source, Lebanese cuisine can be quite low in cholesterol. Our cuisine is based on eating what's in season—lots of legumes, grains and vegetables with spices, aromas, and flavors that are rich and fragrant, and relatively low in cost, providing high quality nutrition with complementary proteins. And although many of our recipes are labor intensive, many are healthy *and* very simple to prepare. But health is only part of the appeal. There is a spiritual component as well. Lebanese tradition uses resources carefully, prepares what is in season locally and, above all, shares. Mother continues to speak of the most important ingredient when she says, "Dear, if you make it with love, it will be delicious."

LIFE IN DOUMA

Douma, a small, beautiful village high in the mountains of north Lebanon, was the birthplace of my mother, Alice Ganamey, in 1910, and of my father, Elias Sawaya, in 1895. Terraced olive trees, apple orchards, *arishes,* grape arbors abundant with grapes, conform to the steep mountainous land that overlooks the Mediterranean Sea, three thousand feet below. To the north, across the *wadi,* a notable geologic formation juts out and up from the earth, paralleling Douma and creating a background to the village so, as one turns the bend from the mountain road above, a most picturesque sight fills the heart. The same geologic formation can be seen from the north in a mirror-image looking across the Qadisha valley from Khalil Gibran's village of Bcharre.

Red tile roofs on hand-cut stone houses line the hill town above the valley. Kitchen gardens with parsley, *baqleh*, mint, onions and chard nestle beside homes. Douma was a cultural and commercial center at the turn of the century. Mama proudly recounts "We had a paved street from cobblestones—the *souk*. It was the best town in 10 miles! With a good store selling fabrics that came from France." In fact, very few towns in Lebanon had cobblestone streets such as Douma. Brass, copper and stainless steel utensils were made by the Douma *haddad*, blacksmith. Douma was called Douma *il Haddeed*—Douma, the iron town, because there were iron mines nearby. Fine furniture was carved by local woodworkers. Plays were performed in Douma, as well as Beirut and Tripoli, and traveling entertainers came through town. A photographer lived in Douma and took formal portraits of Mother and her brothers when they were children, and other families as well.

A restaurant in Douma owned by Isshac l'Hage, mom's great uncle, and *Sitto* Sharife's brother, was famous for the best *hommous* around; people came from neighboring towns of *Tartaj* and *Bchaale* to eat there. Mama recalls that food was served in wooden dishes on little tables, and guests dined seated on the wooden floor.

My grandmother, *Sitto* Dalal, an exceptional cook and mother, survived fourteen years, from 1912 to 1926, of single parenting, the First World War, and food rationing while raising her three young children. Knitting, embroidery, sewing and crochet came easily to her and she followed the custom of making fine lingerie. Her daughter and granddaughters learned these crafts and the art of food. *Sitto* taught us about recycling and conservation of energy as did Mother and Dad. When rinsing rice in the kitchen sink, *Sitto* picked up every single grain that may have fallen out of the strainer, letting nothing go to waste. She collected rubber bands and rinsed out the newly introduced plastic bags of the 1950s. To my mother's dismay, I still do this.

In 1917 there was a tremendous earthquake in Lebanon which Alice remembers well; she was playing at her neighbor's when it happened. Mama tells the story of Dr. Salim Beik Bashir who was visiting her hillside home that had a high balcony overlooking their gar-

den and the *wadi*, valley, below Douma. When the tremor began, it was so forceful and Dr. Bashir was so terrified, he ran out to the wrought iron balcony and was about to jump from the more than two-story height. *Sitto* and her visiting women friends shouted at him to stop, which he did. Eventually the tremor came to a halt; both he and the handcarved stone building with the red tile roof survived.

And Mama, too, lived through this historical event as well as a swarm of locusts, the First World War, hunger and other difficulties. She remembers going to the spring, *ein*, to get water in the evening and visit with friends as they stood in line for the water. In the dry season, the springs flowed slowly, so there was time for much talk. She'd carry water in a *jarra* from the springs at the top of the village, *ein al fou'a*, the one in the middle that dried up long ago, or the one below, *ein at'tahta*.

Mother remembers feeding mulberry leaves to silkworms being commercially raised in a neighbor's home. Um Rashid rented sections of racks in a special room to village women so they could raise their own silk worms. *Sitto* rented a section to keep silk worms and Mama collected mulberry tree leaves to feed them. The worms started as tiny eggs, like seeds, *bizr*, and then hatched into larvae and began to grow, eating lots of mulberry leaves, which Mother cut into shreds they could eat. The worms continued to grow and grow to several inches long. Then they climbed the tumbleweeds placed alongside the racks and each magically spun a silk cocoon. *Sitto* made exquisite applique art pieces with silk cocoons, paid Um Rashid with some, and sold others to silk factories in Batroun or Trablos—a thriving Lebanese cottage industry beneficial to many.

Mama learned French along with her native Arabic in the village school. Alice's father, Dr. Anton Ganamey, our *Jiddo*, a remarkable person, fluent in eight languages, founded the first pharmacy in Douma with his brother Halim. *Jiddo's* name is etched into a marble stone that was perhaps the beam across his pharmacy door. This

ALICE'S KITCHEN

stone sits beside an ancient Roman sarcophagus in the center of Douma bearing the inscription, *"Farmashiyeh Anton Ganamey"*— Pharmacy of Anton Ganamey.

JOURNEY TO AMERICA

After a brief immigration to Mexico and Uncle Adib's birth in 1908, *Sitto* Dalal and *Jiddo* Anton returned to Lebanon where Alice was born in 1910. In 1912, *Jiddo* departed for the United States unaware of the fact that *Sitto* had just become pregnant with their third child, Uncle Edmond, who was born in 1913. *Jiddo* attempted, along with many others who desired to leave behind the hardships of Lebanon, to find the opportunity that America promised. His plan was to practice medicine in the U.S., but since he was a doctor, he was detained in Marseilles for six months, treating American-bound immigrants with trachoma, a then-common eye disease, that prevented their departure until they'd healed.

Finally, *Jiddo* made it to the U.S. and settled in the great Arab-American community of Detroit. World War I began; immigration quotas for "Syrians", as all people from Lebanon, Syria, Palestine were then labeled, prohibited *Sitto* and their children from coming—the start of an enduring legacy of anti-Arab sentiments harbored in the U.S.

Fourteen long years later in 1926, he was able to send for his wife and nearly grown children. Arriving at Ellis Island, they were met by Father Joe Bitar's father, who took them to Detroit, where *Jiddo* had established his medical practice. Alice was 16 and did not speak English; to her embarrassment, she was placed in a class with first graders! She soon became adept with a new language and culture and began to feel at home in Detroit. *Sitto* Dalal assisted Anton with patients since his practice was in their home. Before she learned English, her greeting to patients was "Doctor *bil yensoon"* (the doctor is in the anise) which sounded like the phrase *Jiddo* had asked her to say "The doctor will be in soon."

Dr. Ganamey, an avid reader and lover of books with interests from medicine to metaphysics and art, was a philanthropist and a for-

ward-thinking doctor. In 1928 my grandfather was recognized in an article in Detroit's *Free Press* for saving a stillborn infant's life by injecting adrenaline into its heart. Mother recalls his recommendation of artificial insemination to a couple who were having difficulty conceiving a child. He used acronyms well before his time to facilitate remembering expressions or information, and numerology. His personal journal is a mosaic of art, anatomy, and words of wisdom in many languages, from Ripley's Believe It or Not and *Reader's Digest* to Khalil Gibran.

Jiddo moved his family to California in 1928 to open a clinic. In that fateful year, Alice met a man from her village of Douma, that she would marry in 1934, Elias Jerius (George) Sawaya. Established in California were Elias, his mother, Sharife, his brother, Michael, and his uncle who in 1908 founded the first Melkite church in Los Angeles, Father Gerasimos Sawaya. The big economic crash of 1929 compelled *Jiddo* to return to Detroit with his family after only one year in California, but Elias and Alice had met. He was smitten and travelled to Detroit in pursuit.

In 1934 the marriage took place; Alice moved to Los Angeles with her new husband. *Sitto* came to help for six months after the birth of their first daughter. Three years later *Jiddo* came to Los Angeles for eye surgery, that although unsuccessful, kept them in Los Angeles near their only daughter and her new husband. This was the birthplace of all five daughters: Shirley, Lorraine, Joyce, Vivian, and myself, Linda. I am fortunate to have known *Jiddo*, who taught me

to read and write, and passed on to me his love of books. He lived with us until he died, when I was five years old.

Like many Lebanese, Elias and his brother, Michael, were merchants. They opened a wholesale dry goods store in the early 1920s. Sawaya Brothers Dry Goods was established on Los Angeles Street in the heart of downtown LA's garment district, around the corner from Cole's Famous French Dip Sandwiches, where the sandwiches were memorable and the dill pickles, the crunchiest.

During many rich years of marriage to her husband, Elias, and the raising of five daughters, Mother found time to continue her creativity and handwork with knitting, embroidery, needlepoint, beading, rug hooking, to name a few. Our dear *Sitto* Dalal passed away in 1970. In 1972, shortly after my return from Lebanon, our beloved Elias passed away. He and Mother were planning to visit me in Lebanon in 1971; it would have been their first trip to their homeland since their immigration decades earlier. I waited three months in Beirut, working as a designer. Tragically, Dad became ill, I rushed home, and he died several months later, *allah yirhamu*.

Mother gradually created a new life for herself without her husband. Her passion as an appreciator and collector of fine china and porcelain dolls led her to study ceramics and china painting. Twenty-five years later, in 1997, Alice is 87 years old, with an enthusiasm and infectious vitality that defy age. Her art has flourished over the years, and she continues to innovate and create one-of-a-kind pieces. Included in her repertoire are earrings with fused glass, porcelain desk accessories, figurines, and draped dolls. Mom's passion for learning, creating and sharing with others is an inspiration to those she meets—young and old.

Because of her love of family, tradition, great food, cooking with love and loving to cook, we have her, and those before her to thank for these recipes. Even today, Mother still cooks Sunday dinners, "for the family and whoever can come." Welcome to **Alice's Kitchen**!

Honoring Intuition

Mother's cooking is done intuitively. I have never seen her use a cookbook, though she is literate in four languages. As I recorded our family recipes, her intuitive style proved both a joy and a challenge. Mother would say "Add enough salt" and somehow I knew or learned just how much "enough" was. The fact that we could relate this way showed me how deep our communication had become, because "enough" could mean a dash or a tablespoon or a cup. The challenge then became to transform Mother's instructions into actual measurements. When Mom says "Just put in a heapful teaspoon", I smile at her attempt to be specific in a western way and her charming use of language.

About the Recipes

Most recipes are written as told and as cooked by my family and myself. My goal has been to preserve the simple and more traditional versions of the recipes, as they were made when I was growing up. Cooking evolves with each generation and within generations; thus, Mother's cooking has changed over the past twenty years, since I first recorded many of these recipes. One may detect that we maintain a healthy ongoing discussion about how we cook! I have incorporated some of Mother's changes as well as some of my own, where appropriate.

> PLEASE READ THE FOLLOWING NOTES WHICH PERTAIN TO MOST,
> IF NOT ALL, OF THE RECIPES THAT FOLLOW.

◆ MEASUREMENTS OR HOW MUCH IS ENOUGH?

Our style of cooking is very forgiving, and although I have quantified the recipes, if you do not have enough of what a recipe calls for, in most cases, it is not essential to be precise. Cooking is an art, and the more one cooks, the better one gets, as in any art form. And our individual touches, preferences and differences make us all the more interesting. Mistakes are often our best creations and our greatest teachers, so explore, try variations and make these recipes your own. If your Mother or *Sitto* or Father or *Jiddo* used some spice that you love, that we haven't used, please indulge yourselves!

◆Sᴀʟᴛ

In many recipes, the amount of salt has been reduced for health's sake. It is up to each cook to do what is comfortable and go further in reducing salt, if desired. As Mother says "You can always add more." Our recipes frequently suggest "taste and adjust", so start with a little and add more if it is needed. We both use sea salt in our cooking and olive curing. An alternative to using salt in our traditional way of mashing garlic into a paste is to use citric acid, see below, ʟᴇᴍᴏɴ ѕᴜʙѕᴛɪᴛᴜᴛᴇѕ.

◆Bᴏᴜɪʟʟᴏɴ

Although Mother has been using chicken or beef bouillon granules in some of her cooking, it is not included in the recipes because it adds salt and unnecessary chemicals, such as MSG. Mother describes in her own words how she uses bouillon on page 68.

◆Fᴀᴛ

Some recipes specify clarified butter *or* olive oil; clarified butter is preferable and the only option according to Mother; olive oil is an acceptable substitute, however, especially if there is concern about intake of saturated fat.

◆Fʟᴏᴜʀ ᴀɴᴅ ʀɪᴄᴇ—ʙʀᴏᴡɴ ᴏʀ ᴡʜɪᴛᴇ

In bread baking, a combination of organic whole wheat flour and unbleached white flour is my preference. Mama has always added wheat germ with white flour to increase its nutritional value. Organic brown rice or brown basmati rice rather than the traditional white rice is primarily what I use, but occasionally, white basmati rice is what my mood calls for. Mother uses Mahatma Indian extra long white rice for stuffing or *riz m'falfal.*

◆Oʀɢᴀɴɪᴄ

Organic, homegrown vegetables and grains are preferred, have more nutrition, and less chemicals than commercially grown, rather, manufactured foods. Mama still keeps a vegetable garden and I have been doing so for the past 20 years. By chance, I heard a song on the radio today whose lyrics were "two things you can't buy are love and homegrown tomatoes!" Amen!

◆Mᴇᴀᴛ

If you are carnivorous, meat and fowl from free-ranging, nonsteroid injected animals, are preferable to commercially raised and pro-

cessed products. There is a great difference in eggs from chickens that are raised out of doors and those of factory chickens—if you have ever tasted farm fresh eggs, you know what I mean—and of course, this is the old country way. Before preparing any lamb recipes, please read about lamb, pages 67-70.

◆LEMON SUBSTITUTES

Lemon juice may not always be available or in season, and might add too much liquid to a recipe (such as in spinach pies), so our people use citric acid and other tart seasonings as lemon substitutes. The recipes here are written with lemon juice, but Mother and I both use citric acid frequently instead of, or along with, lemon juice. When making garlic paste, citric acid works well instead of salt to mash garlic into a paste, or can be used in conjunction with the salt, to reduce the amount. Lemon substitutes in Lebanese cuisine are citric acid, sumac in *tabbouli* and *fattoush,* and *hesroum,* sour green grapes mashed and strained in *hommous* and *baba ghannouj,* an old country technique that sounds worth trying. Following is an approximate measurement for substituting citric acid.

1/4 TEASPOON CITRIC ACID EQUALS 2 TABLESPOONS OF LEMON JUICE

◆CLEANLINESS

Mother and *Sitto* were justifiably conscientious about cleanliness. Of course, it is important to rinse all vegetables, pick over grains, rinse and drain them. Clean chicken by rubbing with baking soda and salt and then rinsing well. Rinse fish in water before preparing. Another significant aspect of cleanliness in our cooking, is the extent to which we use our hands to make and form foods. Careful hand-washing prior to and through the process of meal preparation is essential to healthful and delicious meals. If you prefer to use spatulas, food processors or bread machines for kneading dough, these are options. But we love to get our hands in there and create.

Sallem dayetkoom! God bless your hands! Enjoy and *sahteyn!* and much pleasure to you from our collective efforts in these recipes and the fruits of your time spent with love and joy in the kitchen creating them.

Mezza

Mezza—tiny plates of Lebanese traditional delicacies—are served as appetizers with beverages while dinner is simmering and guests arrive. *Mezza* can be an entire meal—an array of finger foods, enticingly sliced vegetables and fresh herbs, or dips with snippets of bread festively set out. Here's a list of ideas; recipes for most follow. For *mezza*, anything goes. For beverage ideas, see that section.

• FRESH CUT VEGETABLES AND SALADS

radishes, carrots, celery, romaine lettuce leaves, Armenian cucumbers, *miiti*, fresh mint, thyme, bell pepper, tomatoes, *tabbouli*, yogurt and cucumber salad, *fattoush, ful akhdar*, green fava beans

• DIPS & COOKED VEGETABLES

hommous, baba ghannouj, batinjan m'tabbal, ful m'dammas, fried eggplant, squash fritters, khudra mahkluta, sautéed veggies

• ENTRÉES

grape leaves, *kibbe nayeh, kibbe bil sineyeh, malfouf mihshi, falafel, sambusik*, meat or spinach pies, *fatayir*

• CHEESE

a variety of cheese from home made to processed such as *jibn*, feta, *ashawan*, or kasseri, *labne* with *zeit, laban*

• BREAD

Arabic bread, *khoobz, tilme b'zaa'tar*, crackers

• PICKLES AND OLIVES

liffit, pickled turnips*, zeitune*, black and green olives, pickles, *makboose, schmandar*, pickled beets

• NUTS AND PRESERVES

pistachios, *fistook*, roasted almonds, cashews, peanuts, Jordan almonds, pumpkin seeds, roasted garbanzo beans, *aadami*, fig jam

Olives

Olives ripen from August through February depending upon the climate and elevation. Green olives are olives picked before ripening to black, still green and on the tree. For successful processing, these need to be opened, by scoring each one with a knife or by the quicker method of pounding them with a mallet. On a trip to Lebanon in the fall, my cousin Elie served fantastic just-picked green olives with savory, cured only four days.

When olives are deep, rich, and purple-black in color, they are ripe for picking and processing without scoring, the type I grew up eating in Los Angeles, *zeitune makboose*. A big sheet was positioned under the tree in our front yard to collect the falling olives. Since we no longer have olive trees of our own, Mother and I have been picking black, ripe olives rather than ground-gathering them. Olives that are picked tend to be firmer and more pungent, without the wrinkles of older fruits that are beginning to dry out.

A great amount of salt is used in this processing. It draws out the bitterness that makes an olive picked from a tree inedible. The salt also functions as a preservative, along with lemon juice and citric acid in the brine. The longer olives are stored in brine, the weaker their flavor becomes; keep this in mind when deciding to put them into jars. Vinegar or lime is used in the brine by some families, while we prefer lemon juice. Experiment with your own variations!

Here is an old country method of determining the correct salt content of the brine. Fill a jar with water and add salt to it. When it has thoroughly dissolved, place a raw egg in the jar. Continue to add salt slowly; the egg begins to rise to the top when the salt to water ratio is correct for preserving olives! About 2 tablespoons per pint is the ratio that floated the egg in the test I performed using sea salt. It's a good idea to boil the water first to remove chlorine and other impurities.

Zeitune Marsouse
GREEN OLIVES
◆

fresh green olives
olive oil
salt
water
lemon juice or citric acid
oregano

1.   In the late summer or fall before olives ripen, pick green olives and crush with a mallet or slit each one with a knife.
2.   Sprinkle with enough salt to coat olives. Mix. Lay on several layers of clean, old, cotton sheets and spread out to dry in the sun, if possible or otherwise indoors.
3.   Mix once a day for 4 to 10 days, adding a little more salt every day. Beginning the fourth day, taste. When no longer bitter, pack olives in jars with fresh oregano, 1 tablespoon salt, 1/2 cup lemon juice or 1 teaspoon citric acid, a little water, and olive oil to cover the olives.

Zeitune Akhdar

GREEN OLIVES

◆

fresh green olives
olive oil
salt
water, boiled and cooled
lemon juice and/or citric acid
oregano or thyme

1. Slit olives and pack into sterile jars. Coat with olive oil, add two tablespoons of salt and fill with water to several inches from the top.
2. Add 1/2 cup lemon juice per quart or 1 teaspoon citric acid; add more olive oil to cover 1/2 inch at the top. Allow to cure for a few weeks.

Zeitune Makboose

BLACK OLIVES

◆

Deep, purple black shiny olives cured in the straightforward old country style—a jar our kitchen counter seemed bare without. What you'll need to make these memorable, flavorful olives: old, clean cotton sheets and a big tray to spread olives on—a surface that won't be damaged by moisture or salt. In the damp Northwest where olives don't grow, I use large, flat woven baskets. But I remember deep enamel pots filled with olives sprinkled with salt that Mom and *Sitto* cured in our warm, dry Southern California kitchen. In such a desert-like climate, it was possible to cure them in a deep pot and just pour off the water drawn out by the salt. *Mabrouk* to your success!

 1 gallon olives
 1 cup salt, approximate
 1 cup olive oil
 1/4 cup lemon juice
 1/8 cup citric acid
 water

 1.   When olives are ripened and dropping from the tree, collect them to cure. The best olives are picked from the tree, firm black and shiny.
 2.   Rinse well and place them in an enamel pot adding water to cover them. Soak small olives for four days and large ones for one week, every day rinsing and changing the water.
 3.   On the last day, drain olives and spread them out on several layers of cotton sheets on a drying tray. Sprinkle with salt, about three tablespoons or enough to coat them well and mix.
 4.   Place trays in the sun or a warm dry place for four or more days, depending upon the size and pungency desired. Once a day mix them and add more salt, which draws out the water and bitterness, and prevents mold from forming.

5.   On the fourth day, taste. If they taste good and are just slightly bitter, they are ready to preserve. Place them in jars, add olive oil and shake up the jar to coat them; add lemon juice and/or citric acid, 3 tablespoons salt (to one gallon) and water. Olives preserved this way will last over a year if there is a minimum of 1/2 inch of olive oil, which separates and rises to the top, forming an air barrier that keeps them from molding. Our family uses lemon juice, but vinegar can be used.

Liffit

PICKLED TURNIPS
◆

In this earthy and time-honored Lebanese pickle recipe, white turnips take on the red of the beet and have a mysterious appearance through the dark beet brine in a jar. Their bright pink color adds a marvelous part of the spectrum and a zesty flavor to *mezza, falafel* or any meal. Keep refrigerated and they'll last a long time.

    2 1/2 pounds turnips
    2 small beets
    1/3 part boiled water
    2/3 part white vinegar
    3 tablespoons sea salt
    5 whole peppercorns
    3 red chili peppers, fresh or dry
    3 cloves garlic

1.   Rinse and trim turnips. Cut into thick slices or wedges. Salt and let stand for several hours to drain.
2.   Slice raw beets. Pack beets, turnips, salt, peppercorns, chili peppers and garlic into a large sterile jar. Fill jar with water and vinegar in above proportions and seal tightly. Allow to pickle for a few weeks, but they can be eaten within a few days.

Ma'kabise

PICKLED VEGETABLES

◆

Pickling has long been used as a method of preserving vegetables for winter use. Try this combination of cauliflower florets, sliced carrots and onions, with garlic cloves, hot peppers, and tiny Armenian cucumbers left intact. Serve with meals or as appetizers and keep refrigerated once pickled.

> 3 pounds mixed sliced vegetables
> 1/4 part boiled water
> 3/4 part white vinegar
> 2 tablespoons sea salt
> 2 tablespoons sugar
> 5 whole peppercorns
> 3 whole chili peppers
> 4 whole garlic cloves

1. Rinse and trim vegetables into relatively even sizes.

2. Place into large sterile jars with salt, sugar, garlic, peppers and spices. Fill jars with water and vinegar in above proportions. Allow to pickle for three weeks, but you may taste them in a few days. Once pickled, store in the refrigerator.

Haleeb

◆

Cheese, Yogurt & Butter

Jibn

ARABIC CHEESE

◆

Simply delicious and easy to make, this fresh cheese was a staple at our breakfast, lunch, *mezza* and dinner table, a perfect complement to olives, both eaten wrapped in snippets of Arabic bread. Cheesecloth and a colander or a fine strainer are used in making *jibn*, which is a soft, unripened Neufchatel-type cheese.

> 1 gallon milk, at room temperature
> 1 junket or rennet tablet
> 1 teaspoon salt

1. Warm milk for about 5 minutes over medium heat in an enamel or stainless steel pot.

2. While milk is heating, place junket or rennet tablet into a saucer and crush it into a powder. Blend it with a couple tablespoons of milk and stir it into warmed milk. Remove from heat. Cover and let mixture stand for two hours.

3. Reheat until it thickens and begins to separate and curdle. Continue to stir until the water, whey, begins to clear. Pour into a colander draped with cheesecloth or a fine strainer with a container underneath to collect the whey, which can be set aside and used for making a ricotta style cheese, *arishe*, next page.

4. While curds are still warm, gently scoop out a handful and press together between your palms, squeezing out as much water as possible, at the same time shaping the curds into a flattened round of cheese. When it begins to hold together, set into a glass container and sprinkle with salt. Continue forming remaining curds into 6 or more rounds of *jibn*. This very light and simple cheese keeps for about a week refrigerated in a covered container.

Arishe

RICOTTA CHEESE

◆

A*rishe*, an easy-to-make ricotta-style cheese, is served fresh with a little salt or sweetened with a little sugar and eaten with Arabic bread. Lebanese pastries such as *knafe b'jibn* and *atayif* use *arishe* sweetened with sugar and flavored with orange flower water— heavenly to be sure.

    whey remaining from making *jibn*, previous recipe
    1 quart milk
    1/3 cup lemon juice
    salt or sugar to taste

1.   In a deep pot, add milk and lemon juice to whey and bring to a boil over medium heat.

2.   Milk begins separating, curdling and rising to the top. Use a slotted spoon to lift and strain curds from the liquid. Place curds in a glass container adding either salt or sugar, if desired. May be stored in the refrigerator for a few days.

Labne

Yogurt cheese

◆

A tart, excellent substitute for sour cream or cream cheese, *labne* is easily made from plain yogurt—either homemade or commercial—and tastes terrific eaten with Arabic bread. For *mezza* appetizers, spread it in out in a beautiful little plate, add a sprig of parsley and drizzle with olive oil. It is a companion to *kibbe bil sineyeh, waraq 'inab,* and is used in savory pastries. The water content of yogurt is drawn out by the addition of salt, creating a delicious, tart, thick and creamy cheese. Mother has been making it recently without any salt at all. The process requires all day or overnight for the yogurt to drain and a cheese bag. A large coffee filter works, but I haven't tried this method. Instructions to make a reusable cheese bag are below. *Labne* is available as kefir cheese in some natural food stores or as *labne* in Middle East food stores.

> 1/2 gallon *laban,* yogurt
> 1/2-1 teaspoon salt (optional)
> cheese bag *kis*

1. Remove a little yogurt and reserve as starter for your next batch. Mix salt into remaining yogurt.
2. Thoroughly wet cheese bag, *kis,* and wring out. It's helpful to have a second set of hands here: Hold the bag open and pour yogurt into the *kis.* Tie bag at the top and hang it up over the sink or a bowl to drain overnight.
3. Remove cheese from bag and refrigerate. Drizzle with olive oil before serving.

TO MAKE A CHEESE BAG, *KIS*:

Cut two pieces of thin muslin or white cotton sheeting to make a rectangular bag, 8 x 10 inches. Sew together at the bottom and sides forming a bag with opening at the top. At the top, sew a channel for a drawstring to close the bag and to use as a hanger. Make a drawstring by sewing one or using a piece of string or a shoelace and insert it into the channel. Wash bag before using it.

Laban

Yogurt

◆

Laban is one of the most ancient foods in the Middle East. According to one account, milk held in sheepskin bags on camels in desert climates naturally fermented and was found to be delicious, thus *laban* began to be intentionally made. Easier to digest than regular milk because of its acidophilus content, *laban* helps balance the intestinal flora.

My earliest memory of eating fresh *laban* was for breakfast with crisp Arabic bread, although Mama fed it to all her five daughters as their first food after breastfeeding. One of the mysterious unmarked containers in the corner of the refrigerator invariably contained a precious amount of *laban* saved as starter, *roube,* for the next batch of yogurt. If you don't have starter, ask a friend, as some commercial yogurts are processed in such a way that they will not work; save some of your home-made batch for the next time.

Since our last cookbook edition, one of our readers, Craig Coté, asked about making *roube;* he remembered his grandmother making it. Mother's memory was jogged by Craig's question and sure enough, she recalled the old country way of making a starter! In the process of doing this book, her memories of the old country, from more than 70 years ago, keep flooding back. A piece of bread was placed in a saucer of milk and left on the kitchen counter to sour. In several days, the soured milk and bread were mashed together and added to the heated milk as the starter. Although we have not tried this yet, we thank Craig for writing and asking the question!

Because there are so many variables and making yogurt is such an alchemical process, read the suggestions below to help you make *laban* that successfully suits your taste.

> 1/2 gallon milk (sheep or goat's milk were used in Douma)
> 1-2 tablespoons *roube* (yogurt culture for starter)

1. Simmer milk until it rises and becomes frothy, stirring frequently with a wooden spoon so it does not scorch. Bring it almost to a boil and immediately remove from heat.

2. Cool until you can put your baby finger in and count to 10; this is *Sitto's* tried-and-true-method.

3. Meanwhile, blend *roube* in a saucer with a little milk, removing any lumps. Stir into the cooled milk, immediately pour mixture into a crock, and cover. *Sitto,* Mom, and Dad always made the sign of the cross over the *laban* to bless it and insure that it came out. Now's the time to bless it.

4. Place crock in a warm spot wrapped in wool blankets where it can remain warm and undisturbed for 8-12 hours while the bacterial action happens and the milk is converted into yogurt. Let it sit overnight if made in the evening or, if made in the morning, leave it all day. An amazing and ancient alchemy transforms the milk into *laban*.

5. Refrigerate and remember to save a little of this batch as *roube*, starter, for the next batch.

SUGGESTIONS FOR SUCCESSFUL *LABAN*

•Thickness can be controlled by how long milk is heated, whether you use whole or low fat milk, and how long you've let it set. The longer you heat it, the fatter the milk, and the longer it sets, all make for thicker yogurt.

• Sourness or tartness can be controlled by the temperature at the time the *roube* is added. The warmer the milk, the more sour. If *roube* has been refrigerated for 1 week or more, it will be more tart. If *roube* is fresher, the *laban* will be sweeter. The more *roube*, the more tart the yogurt will become.

• If the yogurt doesn't set

> •the milk may not have been warm enough during incubation

> •the container may have been disturbed

> •the milk may not have been heated enough to kill certain bacteria which inhibit the "yoging"; conversely, if milk is too hot, it can kill the needed bacteria.

> •the culture may not be good. Some commercial yogurts cannot be used for starter because of their processing.

ALICE'S KITCHEN
CHEESE YOGURT BUTTER

Samne m'fatse

CLARIFIED BUTTER

◆

In the old country *samne*, butter that is clarified, much like Indian *ghee*, is used for cooking. Salts, some water content and impurities in the butter are removed in this process and it is less likely to burn. *Samne* that is refrigerated hardens and keeps for quite some time. It is melted for making *baklawa* or other pastries and in *riz m'falfal*. It is good to have some on hand in the refrigerator.

> 1 pound butter
> 1/4 cup bulgar (optional)

1. In a one quart pot, melt butter over medium heat and add bulgar, which absorbs the sediment and makes it easier to pour off the clarified butter. Let simmer for an hour without stirring.

2. A little residue at the top will turn light brown when it's done. Skim and discard this. Set aside butter and cool to lukewarm.

3. Strain clear liquid through fine sieve or cheesecloth draped over a strainer into a container, leaving sediment at bottom to discard. If you haven't used bulgar, just pour clear liquid off as much as possible, without allowing the cloudy sediment to pour.

4. Refrigerate and when the butter hardens, remove the hardened, clarified butter and discard the milky sediment if any remains. Store in a covered glass container in the refrigerator.

Marqat

◆

Sauces

Taratour

TARTAR TAHINI SAUCE

◆

A rich and tasty sauce for fish, chicken, lamb, *falafel* or drizzled over sautéed vegetables, *khudra makhluta*. Without the parsley, this sauce is also the base for *hommous* and *baba ghannouj*.

> 2-3 cloves garlic, chopped
> 1/2 teaspoon salt
> 1 cup tahini (sesame seed butter)
> 1/4 cup warm water
> 1/3-1/2 cup lemon juice
> 2 tablespoons parsley, finely chopped (optional)

In a wooden mortar and pestle, mash garlic with salt into a smooth paste. Spoon tahini into a bowl, stir warm water in which increases its volume. Slowly stir in lemon juice and garlic paste. Stir in the parsley, taste and adjust seasoning and thickness.

Taratour ma Laban

YOGURT TAHINI SAUCE

◆

Our basic *taratour* or tahini sauce, with yogurt in it.

> 2-3 cloves garlic, chopped
> 1/2 teaspoon salt
> 1 cup tahini (sesame seed butter)
> 1/4 cup yogurt
> 1/2 cup lemon juice

In a mortar and pestle, mash garlic with salt into a smooth paste. Spoon tahini into a bowl, stir in yogurt, lemon juice and garlic paste. Taste and adjust seasoning and thickness.

Toum ou Hammid

GARLIC LEMON SAUCE OR DRESSING

◆

Tangy and classic Lebanese, this is our most essential sauce, dressing, and marinade used with chicken, fish, steamed or sautéed vegetables, potatoes, *salata*, with tremendous healthful benefits such as liver cleansing.

2-3 cloves garlic, chopped
1/2 teaspoon salt
1/4 cup olive oil
1/4 cup lemon juice *or* 1/2 teaspoon citric acid

In a wooden mortar and pestle, mash garlic with salt and citric acid into a smooth paste. Add lemon juice and olive oil. Taste and adjust flavor by adding more garlic, salt, lemon or oil, to suit your taste.

Laban ou Toum

YOGURT GARLIC SAUCE

◆

This yogurt-based sauce is used on various dishes including *ghamme*, rice, potatoes, chicken, or lamb.

2-3 cloves garlic, chopped
1/2 teaspoon salt
1 cup yogurt
1/4 cup white vinegar

In a wooden mortar and pestle, mash garlic with salt into a smooth paste. Stir in yogurt and vinegar. Taste and adjust seasoning, to your taste.

ALICE'S KITCHEN

SAUCES

Toum ou Zeit

GARLIC SAUCE OR MAYONNAISE

◆

This Lebanese version of the Spanish *aioli* or the Italian *agliolio*, garlic mayonnaise, is fabulous on grilled chicken or sautéed vegetables. Vegetable oil thickens more successfully than olive oil. A little olive oil may be added for flavor after mayonnaise thickens.

10 cloves garlic, peeled
1 cup vegetable oil
1/2 teaspoon salt
2 tablespoons lemon juice
dash cayenne pepper

Put garlic, salt, cayenne pepper and lemon juice in food processor or blender and purée. Very, very slowly—this is the secret—drizzle oil into mixture, continuing to blend. As this blends, it thickens becoming a creamy mayonnaise irresistible for dipping.

Zaa'tar Sauce

ZAA'TAR SAUCE

◆

One of many foods eaten with bread at the Lebanese breakfast table, the herb mixture, *zaa'tar* was thought of as a mind-opening food, because of its healthy ingredients. If it isn't baked on thick bread, *tilme*, the sauce is simply served for dipping with bread.

1/2 cup *zaa'tar* mixture
1/4 cup olive oil, *zeit*
1 tablespoon sesame seeds
1/2 tablespoon sumac

Mix ingredients together. Dip with bread or use for topping on *manaishe* or *tilme b'zaa'tar*.

Shourba

◆

Soups

ALICE'S KITCHEN

SOUPS

Shourbat Addis

LENTIL SOUP

◆

Mother's classic lentil soup, so delicious.

6 cup water or vegetable stock
1 cup lentils
1 onion, chopped
2 cloves garlic, minced
1 tablespoon olive oil (optional)
2 celery stalks, chopped
2 potatoes, diced
1/3 cup lemon juice
1/2 teaspoon salt
1/4 teaspoon black pepper
dash cayenne pepper
1-2 cups chopped spinach *or* chard leaves (optional)

1. In a large covered soup pot, bring to a boil and then simmer together the water, lentils, onion, garlic, olive oil, celery, and potato for 1 hour.
2. Add salt, pepper, cayenne, lemon and chard or spinach. Simmer until lentils are cooked. Taste and adjust seasoning.

Shourbat Addis ou Hammid
LEMONY LENTIL SOUP WITH CHARD
◆

Down the hill, nestled in the valley below Douma, the town of Kfar Hilda sits beautifully backgrounded by the distant, blue Mediterranean Sea. On a recent trip to Douma, friends took me to visit Kfar Hilda's ancient Greek Orthodox monastery, Mari Hanna. There, we were graciously served freshly-made blackberry juice, as guests of *Abouna* Touma and *Um* Mariam, who are restoring the monastery that had been damaged by a war-time militia. It is being transformed into a spiritual and temporal oasis that I was blessed to enter. That month, a Romanian icon painter was painting his splendid vision on the chapel's six-foot-thick walls. A few days later I returned there, on foot from Douma, about five kilometers. *Um* Mariam invited me to stay for lunch: this heavenly soup made without *zeit*, oil, as their monastic practice calls for one day a week of their vegetarian diet to be completely fat-free; boiled potatoes with *zaa'tar*, with bread, of course; and their own superb fig jam. I shared a simply divine, memorable meal with the icon painter and a monk. Once home, I created this version to replicate it.

> 6 cup water or vegetable stock
> 3/4 cup lentils, rinsed
> 1 onion, chopped
> 6 cloves garlic, minced
> salt and black pepper
> dash cayenne pepper
> 1-2 cups chopped chard
>   *or* spinach leaves, rinsed, drained and chopped
> 1/2 cup lemon juice

    1.   In a large covered soup pot, bring to a boil and then simmer together the water, lentils, onion and garlic, for one hour.

    2.   Add salt, pepper, and cayenne; continue simmering until lentils are cooked. Add lemon juice and greens. Cook briefly until greens are bright in color and tender. Taste and adjust. Serve hot.

Shourbat Addis ou Rishta

LENTIL AND NOODLE SOUP

◆

1 cup lentils, rinsed
1 onion, finely chopped
7 cups water
1/3 cup olive oil
1/2 teaspoon salt
1/4 teaspoon cayenne pepper
1/4 teaspoon ground cumin
1/4 teaspoon sumac *or* 2 tablespoons lemon juice

NOODLES
2 cups flour
1 cup water
1/2 teaspoon salt

1. Put water, lentils, onion, oil, salt, and pepper into a deep soup pot. Cover and bring to a boil.
2. Reduce heat and simmer for an hour and a half.
3. Meanwhile, make noodles by placing flour in a mixing bowl and mix in salt and water. Knead well, divide into three balls and let stand about fifteen minutes.
4. On a clean, well-floured surface, roll dough out to 1/8 inch thick. Cut into half inch strips by 3 inches long.
5. When lentil soup is almost done, stir in cumin and sumac or lemon juice. Then add noodles a few at a time and cook for ten more minutes, until noodles are done. Taste and correct seasoning. Serve hot with bread and vegetables.

Shourbat Bazella ou riz

SPLIT PEA AND RICE SOUP

◆

1 onion, finely chopped
1/8 cup olive oil
1/4 teaspoon salt
1/4 teaspoon black pepper
1 quart water
1 ham shank (optional)
1 cup dried split peas, rinsed
1/4 cup rice, rinsed
2 stalks celery with tops, chopped
1/4 cup lemon juice

1.   In a deep soup pot, place water, peas, ham shank, onion, olive oil, salt and pepper. Cover, bring to a boil, then reduce heat and simmer for a half hour.

2.   Add rice and celery. Continue to simmer a half hour, stirring once or twice and adding water if necessary.

3.   Lift ham bone from soup and remove ham, adding it to the soup, and discarding the bone. Press soup through a coarse sieve with a mallet or purée in a food processor.

4.   Return soup to the pot, let cook ten more minutes. Add lemon juice at the last minute, taste and add seasoning as needed. Serve hot with crackers.

Shourbat Bazella

Split pea soup

1 onion, finely chopped
1/4 teaspoon salt
1/4 teaspoon black pepper
1 quart water
1 cup dried split peas, rinsed
4-5 whole cloves garlic
1/4 cup rice, rinsed
2 stalks celery with tops, chopped
2 tablespoons lemon juice (optional)

1.　In a large soup pot, place water, onion, peas, garlic, salt and pepper. Cover, bring to a boil, then reduce heat and simmer for a half hour.

2.　Add rice and celery. Continue to simmer 1/2 hour, stirring once or twice and adding water if necessary.

3.　Add lemon juice at the last minute. Turn off heat, taste and add seasoning as needed. Serve hot.

Shourbat Djej ou Riz

CHICKEN AND RICE SOUP

◆

Nutritious and satisfying, this soup is made with either rice or clusters of vermicelli noodles broken up into small pieces and added to broth.

1 whole chicken
1 quart water
2 cinnamon sticks
5 black peppercorns
6 whole allspice kernels
1/2 cup rice *or* 2-3 vermicelli clusters
1 small can tomato sauce
1/2 teaspoon ground cinnamon
1/4 teaspoon black pepper
1/2 cup chopped parsley
1/3 cup lemon juice

1. Rinse whole chicken with water, then rub it with salt and baking soda thoroughly before rinsing well again.
2. Place chicken in a large pot and cover with water. Add several cinnamon sticks, broken in half, allspice, and black peppercorns. Cover and bring to a boil.
3. Skim any residue from top, reduce heat and simmer for 15 more minutes.
4. Remove from heat and remove chicken from broth and set aside to cool. Strain broth and place in clean soup pot. Add rice or vermicelli, tomato sauce, cinnamon, and black pepper to the soup stock. Cover and bring to a boil, then simmer 20 minutes or until rice is done.
5. Debone chicken and add to the soup with chopped parsley and lemon juice. Cook for ten minutes more and serve hot with crackers.

ALICE'S KITCHEN

SOUPS

Shourbat Khudra ma Djej

CHICKEN VEGETABLE SOUP

◆

1 chicken back, neck and wings
2 quarts water
2 cinnamon sticks
5 peppercorns
1 onion, chopped
3 stalks celery, chopped
4 cups chopped mixed vegetables (fresh or frozen
  carrots, corn, string beans, peas, lima beans)
2 potatoes, diced
1 quart whole tomatoes, chopped
  or 1 small can tomato sauce
1/2 teaspoon salt
1/2 teaspoon black pepper
1/4 teaspoon ground cinnamon
2 tablespoons lemon juice
1/2 cup parsley, chopped

1. Rub chicken parts with baking soda and salt. Rinse well and place in a large soup pot, with water, cinnamon, and peppercorns. Cover and bring to a boil. Reduce heat and simmer for fifteen minutes.

2. Remove from heat and strain broth into a clean pot. Set aside chicken. Add all vegetables, tomato, salt, pepper, and cinnamon. Cover and bring to a boil.

3. Reduce heat and simmer for an hour. Meanwhile, remove chicken from bones and discard them. Just before serving, add chicken, lemon juice and parsley to soup and heat through. Serve hot with crackers.

Shourbat Laham ou Riz

LAMB, TOMATO AND RICE SOUP

◆

1/2 pound ground lamb
1/2 teaspoon cinnamon, divided
1/2 teaspoon salt, divided
1/2 teaspoon black pepper, divided
2 tablespoons clarified butter
4 cups water *or* vegetable stock
1/2 cup rice
1 small can tomato sauce
dash cayenne
1/2 cup parsley, chopped

1. Mix lamb with half of the cinnamon, salt, and pepper. Roll into balls about the diameter of a quarter.
2. Heat clarified butter in a deep soup pot. Add lamb and gently brown, stirring frequently.
3. Add water, rice, salt, pepper, cinnamon, cayenne and tomato sauce. Cover and bring to a boil. Lower heat and simmer until rice is cooked, about 20 minutes. Stir in chopped parsley, taste and adjust seasoning. Serve hot.

Shourbat Mahlouta

MIXED BEAN AND GRAIN SOUP

◆

Thick and porridge-like, this is a hearty soup made with a combination of each kind of bean or grain on hand in your pantry. A *kamshe*, small handful, of grains and beans listed below or any others you have or like, slowly cooks into a nutritious, protein-rich soup. The more variety, the richer it will be.

> 7 cups water
> 1 1/2 cups mixed beans and grains
>> 1 tablespoon of each: *ammah* (wheat berries),
>> bulgar, lentils, brown rice, white rice, split peas,
>> black beans, small fava beans, garbanzo beans,
>> red beans, pink beans, white beans, pinto beans,
>> barley, whole dried corn
> 2 onions, chopped
> 2 cloves garlic, minced
> 1/8 cup olive oil
> 1 1/2 teaspoon salt
> 1/2 teaspoon black pepper
> 1/8 teaspoon cayenne pepper
> 1/3 cup lemon juice (optional)

1. Rinse grains and beans. Place all ingredients in soup pot with water and bring to a boil.
2. Lower heat and simmer for one and a half to three hours, until grains are cooked, stirring frequently and adding water if needed.
3. Just before serving, add lemon juice, taste and adjust seasoning. Serve hot with bread, cut fresh vegetables and olives.

Shourba Kibbit Hilli

VEGETARIAN *KIBBE* SOUP

◆

A meat grinder, food mill, or food processor is necessary to create this old family recipe that is very healthy and filling.

4 potatoes, boiled and peeled
1 cup fine #0 bulgar, *burghul*, rinsed and drained
1/2 cup flour
1/2 teaspoon salt
1/2 teaspoon black pepper
1/2 teaspoon ground cumin
1 onion, quartered
1/2 cup olive oil, for frying
1/4 cup parsley, finely chopped for garnish

1. Make basic lentil soup (page 41), omitting celery, potatoes, spinach or chard and olive oil.
2. While soup is cooking grind above ingredients, except for olive oil and parsley, into a large bowl and mix well. Form into balls about the size of a walnut. Heat oil in frying pan and sauté potato balls until golden brown.
3. When lentils in soup are tender, add sautéed balls to soup and cook for about five minutes more. Garnish with chopped parsley and serve.

Shourbat Kishk

KISHK SOUP

Kishk is a traditional Lebanese food made by villagers in the summer for winter use that can be purchased in Middle East grocery stores. Made of *burghul*, bulgar, combined with yogurt, *laban*, it is laboriously ground by hand into a coarse flour called *kishk*. This recipe is for a winter soup which can be made with potatoes instead of lamb as a vegetarian version, both using *kishk*, which is available through some Middle East import stores.

> 2 tablespoons clarified butter
> 1 onion, finely chopped
> 1/2 pound ground lamb
> *or* 3 potatoes, peeled and diced
> 1 cup *kishk*
> 1 quart water
> 3 cloves garlic
> 1/2 teaspoon salt
> 1 tablespoon dried spearmint

1. Heat butter in a deep pot. Add onions and sauté until golden brown. Add lamb and brown for 10 minutes, stirring frequently.

2. Stir in *kishk* and cook for 2 more minutes. Gradually add water, stirring constantly to dissolve *kishk*, removing any lumps that form. Continue cooking for fifteen minutes more.

3. Mash garlic into a paste with salt. Stir in dried spearmint and add to the *kishk*. Serve immediately.

Salata

◆

Salads

ALICE'S KITCHEN

SALADS

Tabbouli

LEBANESE PARSLEY, MINT AND BULGAR SALAD

◆

Fresh whole romaine leaves became boats for *tabbouli* when I was little—tidy containers delivering the salad straight to my mouth. We picked up the lettuce filled with *tabbouli,* like the tacos we loved so much from our kindred Mexican culture. Mama tells me that in the old country, young, tender grape leaves were used to scoop up the salad, similar to our use of Arabic bread. In Lebanon, cabbage leaves are presented as *tabbouli* utensils. There are many possibilities to try before resorting to a fork. Authentic Lebanese *tabbouli* has more parsley than any other of its ingredients. Either Italian flat-leaved parsley or curly parsley, finely chopped, accompanied by bulgar, *burghul,* mint, tomatoes, onion, lemon—providing so much delicious nutrition in every bite! *Tabbouli* even tastes great the next day, so if you have any left, don't throw it away—store it in the refrigerator.

For a winter version of *tabbouli,* when fresh garden parsley was not available in our cold mountain village, the Lebanese make *safsouf,* a variation on *tabbouli* with much more *burghul* and only dried mint. See recipe for *safsouf,* following this.

1/4 cup #1 bulgar, *burghul,* rinsed
    use the smallest grind bulgar available for this salad; if using coarse bulgar, soak it in water for 1 hour and drain prior to using it.
1/4 cup olive oil, *zeit*
1/2 teaspoon salt
1/4 teaspoon cayenne pepper
1/2 cup lemon juice
4 tomatoes, *banadura,* finely chopped
2 bunches parsley, *ba'doonis,* very finely chopped
1 bunch spearmint, *na'na',* finely chopped

ALICE'S KITCHEN

SALADS

1 bunch green onions
   or 1/2 cup yellow onion, finely chopped
1 bunch whole romaine lettuce, cabbage, or young fresh
   grape leaves, for garnish and scooping

1.   Rinse bulgar in a strainer, drain, and place in bowl. Add
olive oil and seasonings to bulgar; set aside to marinate.
2.   Meanwhile, mince parsley, mint and onions; layer them
over the bulgar. Chop tomatoes into 1/2 inch cubes.
3.   Add olive oil and lemon juice and mix well. Taste and
add seasoning as necessary—we love *tabbouli* lemony and tart.
Chill briefly before serving.
4.   Arrange lettuce or cabbage leaves around the perimeter
of a bowl or platter. Place *tabbouli* in the center and serve.

Safsouf

Winter *TABBOULI* Salad

◆

A winter version of *tabbouli, safsouf,* uses much more *burghul,* bulgar, yellow onions rather than green, dried spearmint rather than fresh and includes garbanzo beans which increases the protein by complementing the wheat, bulgar. Neither tomatoes nor parsley are used since they were both unavailable in Douma winters. *Safsouf* is traditionally eaten for lunch with Arabic bread.

1 cup bulgar (#1) the finest size
1/2 cup dry garbanzo beans, soaked overnight
1 onion, finely chopped
1/2 cup whole dried mint leaves
   or 2 tablespoons powdered mint
   or 1/2 cup fresh mint, finely chopped, if available
1/4 cup olive oil
1/3 cup lemon juice
1 tablespoon sumac
1/2 teaspoon salt
1/8 teaspoon cayenne pepper

    1.   Cook dry garbanzo beans in 2 cups of water for 1 hour or until tender.

    2.   Meanwhile, rinse bulgar and drain it. If the bulgar is a coarse grain, soak it in water while the beans are cooking and then drain it. Chop onion and add to bulgar in a bowl along with salt, sumac and cayenne.

    3.   Place drained chick peas on a clean, dry surface. Gently run the rolling pin over them to split them in two. Add them to the bulgar.

    4.   Rub the whole dried mint leaves between your palms over the bowl or add fresh or powdered mint. Mix well and stir in lemon and oil. Toss again, taste and adjust seasoning. Chill and serve.

Fattoush

LEBANESE BREAD SALAD

◆

Another memorable traditional Lebanese salad much less known than *tabbouli*, yet equally fabulous, is *fattoush*. No doubt *fattoush* originated long ago, as did croutons, to use up dry, leftover bread by tossing it into *salata*. Mother heats broken pieces of *khoobz marouq*, Arabic bread, in the oven turned on low for 20 minutes and there it remains overnight to cool and crisp for *fattoush* or to store in a tin for later use. Bread can be toasted quickly in a hotter oven; just keep your eye on it. A delicious variation in *fattoush*—marinating onions in sumac—comes via our friends, the Haddad's from Douma. Their exquisite Lebanese restaurant, Al-Amir, introduced *fattoush* to Portland and sumac in *fattoush* to me, which gives it another dimension. From Al Anadalou restaurant in the Hamra district of Beirut, is the festive addition of pomegranate.

> 3-4 tomatoes, finely chopped
> 1 medium cucumber, quartered lengthwise and sliced
> 3 green onions, finely chopped
> 1/2 head romaine lettuce, chopped
> 1 cup parsley, finely chopped
> 1/2 cup fresh spearmint, finely chopped
>   *or* 2 tablespoons dried spearmint
> 1/2 cup celery and celery tops, finely chopped
> 1/2 cup *baqleh*, purslane (optional)
> 1/2 cup sumac onions (optional, see recipe below)
> 2 loaves of crisp dried or toasted Arabic bread
> 1/4 cup pomegranate seeds (optional)
> 1/2 teaspoon salt
> 1/4 teaspoon black pepper
> dash cayenne pepper
> 1/4 cup olive oil
> 1/3 cup lemon juice

1. Put chopped tomatoes, greens, cucumbers, and onions into a large bowl. Break Arabic bread into bite-sized pieces over cut vegetables and add pomegranate seeds.

2. Drizzle oil slowly and evenly over the bread, then add salt, pepper and lemon juice. Toss and set aside for 5 minutes before serving so bread can marinate and soften slightly. Taste and adjust seasonings. Serve within 10 minutes so bread doesn't become soggy.

Bassle ou Summaq
ONION WITH SUMAC MARINADE
◆

During the months when lemons are not in season, tart tasting sumac may be used as a substitute. When combined with onions and allowed to marinate, the sumac transforms the raw onion, removing its sharpness and bite; the mixture adds a tartness to *tabbouli* or *fattoush,* replacing lemon juice with sumac's own unique red zesty flavor. Beyond adding it to salads, *bassle ou sumac* is an excellent garnish for other dishes such as *falafel, hommous, laham mishwi,* and is tasty simply eaten with bread.

1/2 Spanish onion, julienne cut
2 tablespoons sumac

Toss sliced onion with several tablespoons of sumac in a small bowl and set aside several hours before using. That's it.

Salatat Banadura Elias
MY FATHER'S TOMATO SALAD

◆

Days when my mother wasn't around were a special treat because my father, Elias, would make us lunch. His specialty was this tomato salad, which tasted best in the summer, when made with garden-picked tomatoes. It is laden with garlic, so eat it with friends. The bite-sized chunks of tomato are scooped up with Arabic bread or french bread that absorbs some of the juice. Serve with feta cheese and olives for a perfect summer picnic. Thanks, Dad!

3 cloves garlic
1/2 teaspoon salt
5 garden-ripened tomatoes
1/8 cup olive oil
1/2 bunch fresh spearmint, stemmed, finely chopped
3 rounds of Arabic bread

1.   Peel and chop garlic. In a bowl, mash it into a paste with salt. We like using a wooden mortar and pestle. Cut tomatoes into bite-sized pieces and add them with their juice to the bowl.
2.   Add olive oil and spearmint; toss. Marinate for at least 15 minutes, if possible. A half hour in the refrigerator is perfect. Taste with bread and correct seasoning.

Salata

REAL LEBANESE SALAD
◆

1 clove garlic
1/2 teaspoon salt
1/4 cup lemon juice
2 tablespoons olive oil
3 large salad tomatoes, chopped
2 cucumbers, thinly sliced
8 sprigs mint, finely chopped
6 sprigs parsley, finely chopped
3 sprigs *baqleh* (purslane) optional, stemmed
1 green onion, finely chopped
dash black pepper

1.   Peel and chop garlic. In a bowl, mash it into a paste with salt. Stir in lemon juice and olive oil.
2.   Place chopped vegetables in a deep bowl. Toss with dressing and add a little black pepper. Taste and adjust seasoning. Enjoy with black olives, feta cheese and Arabic bread.

Salatat Alice

ALICE'S SALAD

◆

Alice's *salata* is the one Mother makes most frequently and is more like salads in America because of the lettuce and celery, which are not as common in Lebanon. Serve with *m'jaddrah*, other dishes, or just on its own, it is basically delicious.

2 cloves garlic
1/2 teaspoon salt
1/3 cup lemon juice
1/4 cup olive oil
1/2 bunch romaine lettuce, chopped
3 large salad tomatoes, chopped
2 cucumbers, thinly sliced
2 stalks celery with tops, chopped
2 green onions, chopped
8 sprigs mint, finely chopped
6 sprigs parsley, finely chopped
3 sprigs *baqleh,* purslane leaves (optional)
black pepper

1. Peel and chop garlic. In a bowl, mash it into a paste with salt. Stir in lemon juice and oil.
2. Place chopped vegetables in bowl. Toss with dressing and add a little black pepper. Taste and adjust seasoning.

Laban ou Khyar

YOGURT AND CUCUMBER SALAD

◆

Cool and refreshing in the summer, this native Mediterranean salad with its Asian counterparts from Greek *tzatziki*, to Indian *raita*, is a perfect complement to spicy meals any time of the year. We always peeled the waxy store-bought cucumbers, but home-grown fresh cucumbers just need to be rinsed.

2 cloves garlic
1/2 teaspoon salt
2-3 cucumbers, peeled or not, thinly sliced
1 pint plain *laban* (yogurt)
2 tablespoons dried mint leaves
1 teaspoon lemon juice

1.   Peel and chop garlic. In a medium sized bowl, mash it into a paste with salt. Add cucumbers, *laban,* and garlic. Mix well. Crush the mint into a powder between your palms over the mixture, removing any stems.
2.   Add lemon juice; mix, taste and adjust seasoning.

Salatat Batata

LEBANESE POTATO SALAD

◆

A perfect potato salad with fresh green mint, parsley and lemon. Served warm, at room temperature or chilled, our visually appealing salad complements fish, green vegetables, kebabs or soups and is a delightful change from creamy potato salads.

> 4 medium potatoes, rinsed
> 1/2 cup parsley, finely chopped
> 1/3 cup mint, finely chopped
> 1/3 cup chopped green onions
> 1/2 teaspoon salt
> 1/4 teaspoon black pepper
> dash of cayenne pepper
> 1/8 cup olive oil
> 1/3 cup lemon juice

1. Boil whole potatoes until they are tender, for about 30 minutes in water.
2. Lift them out of the water and set them aside to cool, reserving the cooking water for use as soup stock.
3. When potatoes are cool enough to handle, peel, dice and put them into a bowl. Add chopped greens, seasoning, olive oil and lemon juice, and mix well. Taste and adjust seasoning. Chill and serve, or serve warm.

Salatat Spanegh
SPINACH SALAD
◆

Healthy year-round, this salad is tart and fresh. It makes a wonderful complement to our potato salads.

1 bunch spinach, torn into bite sized pieces
3 green onions, chopped
1/3 cup lemon juice
1/4 cup olive oil
1/4 teaspoon salt
1/4 teaspoon black pepper
dash cayenne pepper
1/2 cup chopped walnuts (optional)

1. Rinse, drain, and tear spinach into a salad bowl.
2. Peel and chop garlic, place in a small bowl, and mash into a paste with salt. Stir in pepper, lemon juice, oil and walnuts.
3. Pour dressing over greens, toss, taste and adjust seasoning. Serve immediately.

Salatat Malfouf

CABBAGE SALAD OR LEBANESE COLESLAW

◆

Crisp and tangy unlike creamy coleslaw, this salad is light and keeps well for a couple of days refrigerated, even with dressing.

1 large clove garlic
1/4 teaspoon salt
1/3 cup lemon juice
1/4 cup olive oil
1/2 head large cabbage, shredded
1/2 bunch parsley, finely chopped
5 green onions, finely chopped
3 tablespoons dried spearmint

1. Peel and chop garlic. In a bowl, mash it into a paste with salt. Mix lemon and oil with garlic paste.
2. Toss greens together in a medium-sized bowl. Crush dried mint over the top between your palms, removing any stems. Pour dressing over greens and toss. Taste and adjust seasoning. Chill and serve.

Salatat Baqleh

Purslane Salad

◆

Many cultures besides Arabic eat *baqleh*, and consider it more than a weed. Called purslane in English, *baqleh* is an herb that is high in Vitamin C and free for the taking in gardens from Mexico, where the Spanish name is *verdolaga* and is cooked in a stew with meat, to the Pacific Northwest. Its lemony flavor and crisp, succulent leaves make it a zesty and unusual addition to any salad. Here, it is the main attraction.

> 1 large clove garlic
> 1/4 teaspoon salt
> 1/4 cup lemon juice
> 1/8 cup olive oil
> 1 cup purslane, *baqleh*
> 1/4 cup parsley, finely chopped
> 1/4 cup *na'na'* spearmint, finely chopped
> 2 tomatoes, chopped

1. Peel and chop garlic. In a bowl, mash it into a paste with salt. Mix lemon and oil with garlic paste. Put chopped vegetables together in medium bowl.
2. Pour dressing over, toss, taste and adjust seasoning.

Salatat Schmandar
BEET SALAD
◆

Earthy and colorful, beet salad is easy to make and complements many dishes.

1 large clove garlic
1/4 teaspoon salt
1/3 cup lemon juice
2 tablespoons olive oil
3-4 whole beets
2 green onions

1. Steam beets in a little water until tender.
2. While they are steaming, peel and chop garlic. In a bowl, mash it into a paste with salt. Mix lemon and oil with garlic paste.
3. Chop green onions. When beets are done and cool enough to handle, slice them into wedges and place in a bowl. Toss with scallions and dressing. Serve warm or cold.

Laham

◆

Lamb

G*hanme,* sheep, have been grazing our ancestral land for centuries. The role of the shepherd is significant from Biblical times: pastoral mountain scenes, feasts of roast lamb, luxurious and sturdy lamb's wool clothing, and exquisite woven rugs—these all find their source in the venerable lamb. Sheep's milk made delicious *laban,* yogurt, and cheese. The fat stored in the exceptionally large tails of Lebanese sheep was prized in cooking for its flavor and preservative qualities. In the old days, small amounts of lamb were coarsely ground, then slowly simmered with seasonings in the tail fat. When cooled, the lard-like mixture, *ourma* or *deben,* as it was called, preserved the meat for winter use prior to the availability of electricity and refrigeration. This flavorful mixture of meat and lard, *deben* or *ourma,* was added to other dishes imparting a meaty flavor, without actually using much meat.

In the old country, lamb, although used sparingly, was the meat of choice. Goat meat, *anzi*, leaner and less tender, was more affordable and was substituted for lamb in the same recipes. Goat milk was primarily used as a beverage, or for making cheese and *laban*.

Many dishes were developed to use the entire lamb—including brains, tripe, tongue, eyes, testicles. Kidney and liver are eaten raw; the famous raw Lebanese *kibbe nayeh* uses parts of the leg. In the early part of the 1900s, lamb was butchered twice weekly in Douma. Nowadays, the butcher daily butchers lamb and goat meat. In California, Mother and *Sitto* painstakingly cut legs of lamb purchased in supermarkets into appropriate cuts for the dishes they wished to prepare—so important to them was the careful removing of fat that causes the unappealing odor and flavor that westerners associate with lamb. Purchasing pre-packaged ground lamb or mutton results in strong tasting dishes with lamb flavor that is too pungent. To avoid this, purchase cuts of lamb and remove the fat yourself; then you can chop or mince it. If you have a butcher you trust, you can have the butcher remove the fat and grind it for you. If you need only a small quantity, such as a cup or two of lamb: buy lean chops; remove any fat; cut into stew-sized pieces, chop finely, or mince.

WHERE'S THE BEEF?

An alternative is to use ground beef. In the 50s and 60s, we rarely ate beef. *Sitto* and Mother always prepared lamb. Now, Mother uses ground beef more frequently. Here are Alice's words on the subject:

> "In Lebanon we only used lamb meat and cleaned out all the bad fat, which gave the food the strong taste. That took lots of skill, time, patience and preparation. The American people don't like lamb because of the taste of the bad fat left in it. Here beef is more accessible than lamb so people use more beef. Beef has more fat which makes it taste good, but fat is bad for us and we have to cut down for health's sake. We must learn how to use beef in our cooking.

> We are now finding short cuts in cooking and dealing with meats that are good to eat without all the fat. People following the same recipe, will have different tasting food because

of the varying amounts of fat left in the meat. Steero chicken or beef granules are an excellent addition to meat, fowl and soup dishes—about 1 teaspoon per recipe; also using it will cut down the amount of salt added. Use chicken with chicken dishes and beef with lamb or beef dishes.

This is what I have learned from my experience for using beef—I buy the leanest ground round—less than 15% fat for raw stuffing, such as in meat pies, *waraq 'inab, kousa mih-shi*, etc. For some stuffings, I use ground chuck, which has more flavor, and I sauté it lightly in a pan, and then drain the excess fat. I then add chopped onions, Steero beef granules, lemon juice and a little clarified butter and seasoning and continue to sauté until the onion is translucent. The flavor is good and there is much less fat."—Alice

LAMB CUTTING

Following are instructions for cutting lamb, removing "the bad fat" and the uses for major cuts of lamb. Our method results in deliciously seasoned, time-tested dishes. Mother and *Sitto* bought a leg of lamb, shoulder, or breast and cut it into various sizes for particular recipes. They would then freeze it flat in freezer bags so that it thawed quickly for convenient use later.

TRIMMING FAT

There are two basic types of fat: one is moist and smooth which is fine to keep in small amounts; the other type is dry, flaky and chalky—this is to be completely cut away and discarded; it is the fat that is unpleasantly strong tasting.

LEG-CUTTING

LEG—APPROXIMATE YIELD 3 TO 4 CUPS OF LAMB PER LEG

LEAN PIECES BEST FOR *KIBBE, LAHAM MISHWI,* STUFFING *MIHSHI*

    1.   With a sharp meat knife, carefully remove meat from bone. Then cut away and discard veins, arteries, and muscles.

    2.   Set aside large, lean pieces for *kibbe*; large pieces with a little fat are suitable for shish kebab; cut smaller pieces for stew or stuffing. See next page for details on each.

ALICE'S KITCHEN

LAMB

69

- HOW TO CUT LEG OF LAMB FOR SHISH KEBAB, *LAHAM MISHWI*

Cut larger pieces into 2" cubes, leaving on a little moist fat. Set aside smaller pieces for stew or stuffing. Remove and discard gristle and fat that is dry, flaky, or chalky.

- HOW TO CUT LEG OF LAMB FOR FOR *KIBBE*

Cut pieces into 2" cubes, removing all fat. Set aside smaller pieces for stuffing. Remove and discard gristle.

- HOW TO CUT LEG OF LAMB FOR STEW AND STUFFING, *MIHSHI*

Remove and discard all dry, chalky fat and gristle. Cut pieces, leaving a little fat on, into 1" cubes. Cut smaller pieces into 1/4" and set aside for use in stuffing.

BREAST-CUTTING

BREAST—APPROXIMATE YIELD 2 CUPS OF LAMB PER BREAST

FLAVORFUL, MOIST MEAT PERFECT FOR STUFFING, *MIHSHI*, AND BONES FOR STEW

1.   With a sharp meat knife, separate meat from bone, leaving a little meat on the bone for stews, soups, or to place under grape leaves, cabbage rolls or *kousa mihshi*
2.   Section large riblets along cuts begun by butcher.
3.   Cut off flange or flap on remaining end. Skin it, remove fat and discard skin and fat. Remove and discard dry, chalky fat.
4.   Cut in strips and then into 1/4" pieces for stuffing.

SHOULDER

SHOULDER—APPROXIMATE YIELD 2 CUPS OF LAMB PER SHOULDER

USED FOR SHISH KEBAB, *LAHAM MISHWI*, STEW, OR STUFFING, *MIHSHI*

Follow instructions for leg cutting, above and previous page.

M'hamsa

SAUTÉED LAMB FOR STUFFING

◆

M'*hamsa* can be used for stuffing or just eaten with bread. I remember walking by the kitchen stove and not being able to resist scooping up a bit, a *litme,* with a piece of Arabic bread. It is used as cooked stuffing for: *sheikh al mihshi, batata bil sineyeh, kibbe bil sineyeh.*

> 1 1/2 pounds lamb, cut very small or coarsely ground
> 1 large onion, finely chopped
> 1/4 cup pine nuts
> 2 tablespoons clarified butter *or* olive oil
> 1/2 teaspoon salt
> 1/4 teaspoon pepper
> 1/4 teaspoon cayenne
> 1/2 teaspoon cinnamon
> 1/2 teaspoon ground allspice
> 2 tablespoons lemon juice

    1.   Sauté lamb until well done in clarified butter with finely chopped onion, salt and whole pine nuts.

    2.   Season with black pepper, a dash of cayenne, cinnamon, allspice and lemon juice just before cooking is complete. Serve with bread or use for stuffing.

Laham Mishwi

SHISH KABOB

◆

A classic Lebanese dish our family frequently enjoyed in our Los Angeles patio or at *mahrajans* or family picnics—this summer specialty was barbequed along side a few hamburgers (with parsley) and served with Arabic bread and *tabbouli* or *salata* and *batata miqliyyi*, french fries. A cross-cultural feast!

> 1 1/2 pounds lamb, cut in 2 inch cubes (page 69)
> 1 or 2 onions, cut into large pieces for skewering
> 3/4 teaspoon salt
> 1 teaspoon black pepper
> 1 teaspoon cinnamon
>
> 5-7 skewers

1. Mix all of the above together in a bowl, cover and refrigerate for a couple of hours to marinate.
2. Place charcoal in barbeque and light it. While it is heating, place alternating pieces of lamb and onions on each skewer. When coals are hot, barbeque for about 5-7 minutes on each side, being careful not to overcook as meat will toughen.
3. Remove barbequed lamb from skewers by holding Arabic bread in your hand and sliding the *laham mishwi* off. The bread soaks up some of the flavors of the meat and I remember everyone wanted that piece of bread! The barbequed onions, wrapped with a little meat in the Arabic bread made such tasty morsels.

Kafta Mishwiyeh

GRILLED GROUND LAMB

◆

Lebanese cousin to hamburger, our well-seasoned *kafta* is wrapped around a skewer and tastes great grilled or barbequed, served with bread and rice. If you prefer to bake it like a meat loaf, pour lemon and garlic marinade sauce, below, over it for the last 5 minutes of baking.

1 pound ground lamb
1 onion, minced
1/2 teaspoon each salt and black pepper
1/4 teaspoon allspice
dash cinnamon
1/2 cup parsley, finely chopped

TO GRILL, BROIL OR BARBEQUE

1. Mix the above ingredients thoroughly in a bowl. Roll into patties, wrap onto skewers with your hand and shape to a uniform thickness.

2. Grill over coals, for about 4 minutes on each side until done. Remove from skewers by holding Arabic bread in your hand and sliding the *kafta* off. We used to fight over that tasty bread!

TO BAKE

1. Mix the above ingredients thoroughly in a bowl and spread 1 inch thick into a lightly oiled baking tray. Dip your hand in cold water and smooth the surface of the lamb mixture.

2. Bake in a preheated oven at 450°F on the bottom oven rack for 15 minutes. Remove tray from oven and skim any residue that formed. With a sharp knife, cut *kafta* into 3 inch squares and return to oven for 10 more minutes.

3. In the meantime, while it is baking, make the following sauce to add flavor the last five minutes of baking.

Garlic Lemon Marinade

1 clove garlic
1/2 teaspoon salt
1/2 cup lemon juice

In a small bowl, mash garlic with salt, add lemon juice and pour over meat. Broil for 5 more minutes, until browned, and serve immediately.

Kafta bil Sineyeh ou Bazella

LEBANESE MEATLOAF WITH PEAS AND TOMATO SAUCE

◆

1 pound ground lamb
1 onion, minced
1/2 teaspoon salt
1/2 teaspoon black pepper
1/4 teaspoon allspice
dash cinnamon
1/2 cup chopped parsley
1 package frozen peas, for top
1 small can tomato sauce, for top

1.   Mix the above ingredients, except peas and tomato sauce, thoroughly in a bowl. Spread lamb mixture 1 inch thick into a lightly oiled baking tray. Dip your hand in cold water and smooth the surface.

2.   Bake in a preheated oven at 450°F on the bottom oven rack for 15 minutes. Remove tray from oven and skim any residue that has formed. With a sharp knife, cut *kafta* into 3 inch squares.

3.   Spread frozen peas evenly over the *kafta* and then the can of tomato sauce. Return tray to oven, lower heat to 350°F and bake an additional 15 minutes until done.

Burghul M'falfal

LAMB SHANKS WITH BULGAR

◆

2 pounds lamb shanks, rinsed and drained
2 quarts water
3-4 whole cinnamon sticks
1/2 teaspoon salt
6 whole peppercorns
6 whole allspice kernels
1 cup #4 bulgar, *burghul,* rinsed and drained
1/4 cup clarified butter

1. Boil lamb shanks and bones with water, cinnamon sticks, peppers, and allspice for about 30 minutes, until meat begins to loosen from the bone. Set aside to cool.

2. Place *burghul* in a deep pot and brown for a few minutes, stirring constantly, before adding butter. Add clarified butter, stir and continue to brown.

3. Strain broth from lamb shanks and add three cups broth to *burghul.* Cover and steam for 15 minutes. Check and add more broth if needed.

4. Remove meat from lamb shanks, discarding gristle and fat. Add meat to *burghul.* Steam 10 more minutes. Turn off heat and let stand for fifteen minutes before serving with *laban, khoobz,* and carrot sticks.

Kibbe Nayeh

RAW *KIBBE,* MINCED LAMB & BULGAR

◆

In the old days lamb pieces were pounded by hand in a *jirn* to pulverize the meat into a paste, then combined with bulgar, onion, and seasoned with pepper and spices to create this legendary Lebanese dish, often referred to as the national dish of Lebanon. Mother had a fancy electric meat grinder she used to grind the meat with ice cubes in making the *kibbe* that she is famous for and that our family loved. Mama says, "the colder the meat, the better the *kibbe*". Typically served for special guests and celebrations, Mother garnished it decoratively with long green scallions. *Kibbe nayeh* is eaten by scooping up bite-sized portions with Arabic bread. The leftovers are made into a dish that I have, since childhood, preferred to the raw *kibbe*, called *kibbe bil sineyeh,* the next recipe, which is baked and filled with pine nuts or made into *kibbe ros.* My friend, Josephine, tells me a food processor will pulverize the meat so it will have some elasticity for binding with the rest of the ingredients; Mother still uses her meat grinder method, as follows.

1 1/4 cups #1 bulgar

2 large onions, quartered

2 pounds lamb, cut into 2 inch chunks (page 69)

1 tablespoon black pepper

2 teaspoons salt

4 kernels whole allspice, freshly ground
  or 1/4 teaspoon ground allspice

1/4 teaspoon cayenne pepper

1 tray of ice cubes

1 bunch of green onions for garnish

1.   Rinse and drain bulgar. Squeeze excess moisture from bulgar with your hands and put into a large bowl. Grind onions into bowl over bulgar. Add seasonings, mix well and set aside.

2.   Grind meat—either use a meat grinder or have butcher

grind it twice, fine like hamburger. To grind it yourself: Grind meat and several ice cubes through a meat grinder fitted with a coarse blade into a separate bowl. Then grind it a second time with a finer blade, using more ice to push the rest of the meat through.

3.   Mix ground meat very thoroughly with bulgar/onion mixture. Now grind this mixture again with ice. If a butcher ground the meat for you, mix lamb and bulgar together with ice cubes, so the texture is smooth. In either instance, the mixture holds together best when cold and moist. Use more ice to achieve proper texture. Taste and adjust seasoning.

4.   Serve raw *kibbe nayeh* mounded on an oval platter garnished with whole green onions and Arabic bread. Smooth out the surface of the *kibbe* by dipping your hand in cold water and shaping the surface into an oval, domed shape. Mom then takes the back of a fork and presses a design into the surface, pokes a few scallions for garnish into the top with the tips sticking out and parades it onto the table, for this most famous and traditional dish.

Kibbe bil Sineyeh

BAKED *KIBBE* WITH PINE NUTS

◆

K*ibbe bil sineyeh* transforms leftover raw *kibbe nayeh* into an even more savory creation that is filled with pine nuts and baked. Traditionally eaten with *labne* and bread, *kibbe bil sineyeh* can be served hot, warm or cold and the leftovers fried with scrambled eggs in *kibbe ou bayda*. The same basic recipe takes on a different shape in *kibbe ros*: football-shaped balls stuffed with the same filling and baked.

> 1/4 cup clarified butter, cold
> 2 1/2 cups *kibbe nayeh*, see recipe previous page
> 1/2 cup #1 bulgar, *burghul*
> a bowl of ice water for dipping your hands
> 1/2 cup pine nuts
> 1/3 cup olive oil

    1.   Coat the inside of an 8" x 13" tray, or a 12" round baking tray evenly with olive oil. Preheat oven to 400°F.

    2.   Rinse and drain *burghul*; mix thoroughly into *kibbe nayeh* with your hands.

    3.   Wet hands and form half of the *kibbe* into balls. Flatten each ball into a patty about 1/2" thick between your hands and place them on the bottom of the tray completely covering it. Smooth out surface with your hand dipped in ice water, blending the layer so there are no gaps.

4. Rinse and drain pine nuts, sprinkle evenly over surface, and pat down gently. Cut one half of clarified butter into pieces and dot evenly over the pine nuts. Form remaining *kibbe* into balls and patties to cover the filling with another 1/2" thick layer. Smooth out the surface with your wet hand.

5. Cut a decorative pattern into the tray as follows: Cut into lengthwise strips 1 1/2" wide, cutting all of the way through to the bottom of the tray. Make another series of parallel cuts at 45 degrees, also 1 1/2" wide, creating diamond shapes. With the point of a knife, incise the center of each diamond all the way through to the bottom of the tray. Not only is this decorative, it allows for thorough cooking. Use the knife to cut around the edge of the tray to separate the *kibbe* from the pan.

6. Pour olive oil and divide remaining clarified butter evenly over the top. Bake 30 minutes on lower oven rack until edges brown. Move to upper rack and continue baking until top browns. Remove from heat, sprinkle with a handful of water to moisten. Recut diamonds and serve.

Sfeeha or Fatayir

SAVORY PASTRY OR MEAT PIES

◆

Another family favorite, *sfeeha,* are triangular shaped savory pastries filled with lamb, onions and pine nuts and then baked. These disappeared as fast as they hit the dining room table and sometimes only a few made it that far out of the kitchen. The flavors in *sfeeha* become more vivid as they cool and are even delicious eaten cold. A dollop of tart *labne* on top of these perfect finger foods will please your guests. The same basic recipe made in an open-face version is called *laham bil ajeen,* the next recipe. Follow basic bread dough recipe and while it rises, the filling can be mixed.

DOUGH

> follow recipe for basic bread dough (page 162)

FILLING

> 3 cups lamb finely chopped or coarsely ground
> 2 cups onions, finely chopped
> 1/2 cup pine nuts
> 3/4 cup *labne* (page 32)
> 1/2 teaspoon citric acid *or* 1/2 cup lemon juice
> 2 teaspoons cinnamon
> 1/2 teaspoon salt
> 1 teaspoon black pepper
> 2 teaspoons mild cayenne pepper
> > *or* 1/2 teaspoon hot cayenne
> 6 whole allspice, freshly ground

FILLING

1. Cut meat, chop onions and place in large bowl.
2. Add seasonings, pine nuts and *labne*. Mix thoroughly; then add citric acid or lemon juice. Taste and adjust seasoning.

1.   Using a rolling pin, roll out one ball of dough on a well-floured surface to about 1/8" thickness.

2.   Use a mason jar cap (3 1/2" diameter) to cut out as many circles as possible. Put scraps of dough into a bowl; set aside.

3.   Place two tablespoons of filling into each circle and close into a triangle as follows or make flat open-faced pies as directed in *laham bil ajeen,* the next recipe.

FORMING TRIANGLES

•Using your left hand, pull up the dough from 12 o'clock and 4 o'clock on the circle of dough to the center and pinch together and hold.

•With your right hand at the outer edge, pinch edges of dough together all the way to the center of the circle, sealing the edge and forming the first point of a triangle.

•Rotate the pie holding the center with one hand and pull up the midpoint of the remaining dough and pinch towards the center, forming the second point of the triangle.

•Fold in the third point, pinching together but leaving 1/2 inch opening at the center of the pie.

SUGGESTIONS ON FORMING TRIANGLES

• Dust fingers slightly with flour before pinching dough so it will stay together.

• Try to keep the moist filling away from the outer edge of the circle and thus, out of the joint.

•Push dough in at the point of the triangle before pinching closed to keep moisture in the pies as they cook.

4.   Place pies on oiled baking tray or a tray lined with baking parchment allowing 1/4" between each pie. Preheat oven to 400°F.

5.   Knead dough scraps and form into a ball, dust with flour, cover and let rise again to use. If you have extra dough and no more filling, use it to make *tilme b'zaa'tar*, plain *tilme, khoobz*, or a pizza! Another option is to freeze extra dough for later use: just roll it into a ball, then dust with flour, cover tightly with plastic wrap and freeze in a plastic freezer bag.

6.   When baking tray is full, bake pies on lower rack of oven for 15 to 20 minutes or until golden brown on bottom. Move tray to upper rack and bake until top pinched edges are brown, another 10 minutes or so.

7.   Remove from tray and place to drain on open paper grocery bags to absorb any excess oil and to cool. *Sahteyn!*

TO FREEZE PIES FOR LATER BAKING

Place pies on ungreased tray in freezer for several hours until individually frozen and then pack in freezer bags and place in the freezer to store.

Laham Bil Ajeen

Lamb Open-Faced Meat Pies

◆

Almost identical to *sfeeha, laham bil ajeen* is open faced with a quicker cooking time and the addition of a little chopped tomato. Try them both to see which you prefer. Begin with dough, and while it is rising, make the filling for *sambusik* or *sfeeha* filling.

1. Make basic bread dough recipe on page 162, to rising.
2. While dough is rising, follow recipe for filling on page 81, with the meat more finely chopped, or minced. Finely chopped tomato can also be added to the filling for *laham bil ajeen*.

Assembly

1. Using a rolling pin, roll out one ball of dough on a well-floured surface to about 1/8" thickness.
2. Use a mason jar cap (3 1/2" diameter) to cut out as many circles as possible; put scraps of dough into a bowl and set aside. Circles of dough can be larger, like pizza, or shaped into rectangles.
3. Sprinkle dough with a little water and spread one or two tablespoons of filling over each circle to 1/4" from the edge. Since the lamb is uncooked, make the layer of meat no more than 1/4 inch thick, so that the meat cooks thoroughly by the time the dough is done baking. Preheat oven to 450°F.
4. Place pies on oiled baking tray or a tray lined with baking parchment allowing 1/4" between each pie.
5. Knead dough scraps and form into a ball, dust with flour, cover and let rise again. If you have extra dough and no more filling, use it to make *tilme b'zaa'tar*, plain *tilme, khoobz*, or a pizza! Another option is to freeze extra dough for later use: just roll it into a ball, then dust with flour, cover tightly with plastic wrap and freeze in a plastic freezer bag.
6. When tray is full, bake on lower rack of oven until golden brown, approximately 10 minutes. Move to upper rack and bake 5 more minutes, until top crust is golden brown and meat is cooked, about 15 minutes total. Cool and serve.

Alice's Kitchen

Lamb

Sambusik

SAVORY PASTRY

◆

T hese scrumptious savory pastries are very similar to the meat pies we grew up eating, but Mother and *Sitto* didn't make them as often as *sfeeha*. The *sambusik* are richer than *sfeeha* as the dough is made with butter, and they, too, disappear as fast as they are put on the table. Perfect for *mezza* or as a side dish, *sambusik* can be served hot or at room temperature. Filling and dough can be made ahead and refrigerated or the pastries can be made and frozen, then baked or fried later. In Douma, they were usually fried, because people did not have ovens in their homes; today, baking them is recognized as more healthful. Try both methods to discover which you prefer.

DOUGH

    1 cube butter, softened
    4 cups unbleached white flour
    1/2 teaspoon salt
    1/2 teaspoon yeast
    1 cup water

FILLING

    2 cups onions, finely chopped
    3/4 teaspoon salt
    2 tablespoons olive oil
    1/2 cup pine nuts
    1 pound ground or finely-chopped lamb (page 69)

1 teaspoon cinnamon
3/4 teaspoon black pepper
1/2 teaspoon cayenne pepper
6 whole allspice, freshly ground
    or 3/4 teaspoon ground allspice
1/2 cup *labne* (page 32) *or* kefir cheese
2 tablespoons lemon juice

DOUGH

1. Combine softened butter with salt and flour. Mix well by hand to blend completely.
2. Dissolve yeast in lukewarm water and let proof for 5 minutes. Knead yeast thoroughly into flour mixture. Divide and roll into four balls; cover, let rest 1/2 hour while you make the filling.

FILLING

1. Sauté onions and salt in olive oil over medium heat until onions are translucent. Add pine nuts and sauté a few more minutes.
2. Add meat, stirring occasionally for 10 minutes. Just before meat is fully browned, add seasonings and cook two more minutes. Remove from heat, add *labne* and mix well. Cool. Mix in lemon juice, taste and adjust seasoning.

ASSEMBLY

1. Roll out one ball of dough at a time on lightly floured board to 1/8 inch thickness. Cut into circles about 3 inches across with a canning jar ring. Roll dough scraps into a ball and set aside to rest for use if needed; it can also be frozen for later use.
2. Fill each circle with a tablespoon of filling. Fold in half and pinch curved edges in well to seal, forming fat half-moons.

TO FRY

Deep fry in equal parts olive oil, clarified butter and vegetable oil over high heat until golden.

TO BAKE

Arrange pastries on a tray lined with baking parchment. If you wish, brush pastries with melted butter or a little olive oil. Bake in preheated oven at 400°F for 15 minutes on bottom rack, then move tray to top rack for 10 minutes or until browned.

Asabi' bil Lahme Mafroume

FILO DOUGH FINGERS WITH LAMB

◆

Another delightful savory pastry that is relatively simple to prepare and is excellent served as an appetizer or entrée.

> 1 package filo dough
> 1/2 cup clarified butter

M'HAMSA FILLING

> 1 1/2 pounds lamb, minced or coarsely ground
> 1 large onion, finely chopped
> 1/4 cup pine nuts
> 2 tablespoons clarified butter
> 1/2 teaspoon salt
> 1/4 teaspoon pepper
> 1/4 teaspoon cayenne
> 1/2 teaspoon cinnamon
> 1/2 teaspoon ground allspice
> 1 tablespoon lemon juice

FILLING

1. Sauté lamb until well done in clarified butter with finely chopped onion, salt and whole pine nuts.
2. Season with black pepper, cayenne, cinnamon, allspice and lemon juice just before cooking is complete.

ASSEMBLY

1. On a flat tray, brush both sides of each filo leaf with butter as you layer 3 to 5 leaves on top of each other.
2. Place 1 inch of lamb stuffing along one edge of dough and roll into a long tube the width of a cigar.
3. Cut into 3 inch lengths for baking. Repeat until you have used all the stuffing and filo. Bake in preheated at 350°F for 30 minutes or until lightly browned.

Batata bil Sineyeh

BAKED POTATO AND LAMB PIE WITH PINE NUTS

Along the lines of shepherd's pie, *batata bil sineyeh* combines the comfort of potatoes with the delicacy of pine nuts accompanying the savor of a little spiced lamb. Mother's guests love it and frequently ask for the recipe. Start the potatoes cooking first, while you make the filling.

FILLING

    1/8 cup olive oil
    2 large onions, finely chopped
    1/2 teaspoon salt
    2 pounds lamb, minced (page 69)
    1/4-1/2 cup pine nuts
    3/4 teaspoon black pepper
    1/4 teaspoon cayenne pepper
    1/2 teaspoon cinnamon

POTATOES

    10-12 medium potatoes
    1/4 cup milk
    1/2 teaspoon salt
    1/2 teaspoon black pepper
    1 cube butter *or* 1/2 cup olive oil
    1-2 cups bread crumbs

1.   Sauté onions, salt and lamb in olive oil over medium heat until lightly browned, about 15 minutes. Add pepper, cayenne,

cinnamon, and pine nuts and sauté 5 more minutes. Taste, adjust seasoning, and set aside.

2.   Boil or steam whole potatoes in water with one tablespoon milk until tender. Milk, Mama says, brings out the flavor of potato. Drain (reserve for soup stock) cooked potatoes; then peel and mash them while still hot with salt, pepper, butter and remaining milk.

3.   Preheat oven to 350°F and grease 8" x 13" pan.

4.   Moisten hands with milk to keep from sticking, and spread half of the potatoes in the pan. Layer the lamb stuffing evenly over the potatoes. Cover lamb layer with remaining potatoes by making potato patties between your palms and pressing them to completely cover the filling.

5.   Sprinkle top layer with bread crumbs. Bake for 45 minutes until golden brown on top. Let stand for ten minutes before cutting and serving.

Shish Barak

LEBANESE RAVIOLI IN YOGURT SAUCE

◆

DOUGH

    2 cups flour
    1 cup milk
    1/2 teaspoon salt

FILLING

    1 pound ground lamb (page 69)
    2 onions, finely chopped
    1/2 tablespoon clarified butter
    1 cup pine nuts
    1/2 teaspoon cinnamon
    1/2 teaspoon black pepper
    1 tablespoon parsley, finely chopped

SAUCE

    4 cups yogurt, *laban*
    1 egg
    1 tablespoon corn starch
    3 cloves garlic
    1 tablespoon dried spearmint or cilantro

1.   Mix flour with salt in a bowl. Add milk to make dough and knead well and set aside.

2.   Mix filling ingredients together in a bowl.

3.   Roll out dough to 1/8 inch thick and cut into 3 inch circles using a canning jar lid. Place a heaping teaspoon of filling into the center of each circle. Fold in half and pinch edges together to seal. Fold the two corners towards each other, overlapping a little and pinch together to form a hat-like shape, like those in the photo with our cousin Nina Sawaya al-Bacha in Douma.

4.   Place them on a tray and into a preheated oven at 350°F

for ten minutes to dry a little. Remove from oven and set aside.

    5.   To make sauce, put yogurt in a deep pot and beat in the egg and corn starch, stirring well and smoothing out any lumps. Heat over a low flame for ten minutes, stirring frequently.

    6.   Mash garlic into a paste. Stir in dried spearmint and add to the yogurt.

    7.   Drop ravioli into yogurt and cook over low heat for 10 to 15 minutes. At ten minutes, test one to see if they're done, which will vary with the size you have made. Serve hot.

M'farkey

EGGPLANT AND LAMB STEW

♦

Hearty and wholesome, this stew, as many Lebanese stews with meats and vegetables, is served over a bed of rice and eaten with Arabic bread. Rather than salads, a fresh vegetable platter with romaine lettuce leaves, carrot strips, radishes, mint leaves and green onions makes a fine accompaniment and adds contrast.

2 eggplants
3 cups lamb breast, coarsely chopped
    or ground lamb (page 69)
1/2 teaspoon salt
2 tablespoons clarified butter or olive oil
2 large onions, finely chopped
3 cloves garlic, finely chopped
3 large, ripe tomatoes
    or 1 large can whole tomatoes, chopped, with juice
1/2 teaspoon black pepper
1/4 teaspoon cayenne pepper
1/2 teaspoon cinnamon

1. Peel eggplant and cut into 1 1/2" cubes. Salt and place in a bowl or colander to drain.
2. Meanwhile, sauté lamb with salt, onions and garlic in clarified butter, until lightly browned; add eggplant and brown 10 minutes.
3. Add tomatoes, pepper, cayenne, and cinnamon. Cook on medium heat for 5 minutes. Stir gently with wooden spoon so that eggplant doesn't get mashed.
4. Cover, lower heat and simmer for about 45 minutes until eggplant is thoroughly cooked, stirring gently every 15 minutes. Serve hot over *riz m'falfal*.

Riz ou Fassoulia
LIMA BEANS WITH LAMB & TOMATO OVER RICE

◆

Rice and beans, *riz ou fassoulia*, are complementary proteins in this delectable version that brings to mind memories of winter family dinners: ten of us crowded around the dining room table, kids sometimes sitting at the kitchen table because there was not enough room at the big table, and everyone loving the fulfilling flavors that this meal provides. Serve over *riz m'falfal* with fresh cut vegetables or steamed asparagus with lemon and garlic, and, of course, olives and Arabic bread.

2 tablespoons olive oil *or* clarified butter
1 1/2 pounds lamb, cut into 3/4" cubes for stewing
3/4 teaspoon black pepper
1/4 teaspoon cayenne pepper
1/2 teaspoon cinnamon
3 medium onions, chopped
2 cloves garlic, finely chopped
1/2 teaspoon salt
1 can whole tomatoes, chopped, with liquid
2 packages frozen baby lima beans
    or 3/4 cup dry navy beans, soaked overnight

1. Sauté lamb in clarified butter or olive oil with seasonings, until light brown over medium heat. Add onions and salt, continuing to sauté 5 minutes.

2. Add tomatoes, with their liquid, and beans. Cover and simmer for 20 minutes if frozen beans are used. Dry beans, soaked overnight take two hours of simmering to be tender, and could simmer longer.

3. Stir occasionally, adding water if necessary, until beans are done. Serve over *riz m'falfal* with Arabic bread.

ALICE'S KITCHEN
LAMB

Bamyia ou Laham
OKRA AND LAMB
◆

The flavor of okra, *bamyia*, simmered with tomato, onion, garlic, and lamb on a bed of rice and eaten with Arabic bread, carrot sticks and romaine lettuce leaves, is a fine summer supper, when okra is in season.

2 tablespoons olive oil *or* clarified butter
1 1/2 pounds lamb, cut in 1-inch cubes for stewing
3/4 teaspoon black pepper
1/4 teaspoon cayenne pepper
1/2 teaspoon cinnamon
3 onions, chopped
2 cloves chopped garlic
1/2 teaspoon salt
1 can whole tomatoes, chopped, with liquid
1 pound fresh okra

1.   Sauté lamb in clarified butter or olive oil with seasonings, until light brown over medium heat.Add onions, garlic and salt, continuing to sauté 5 minutes.
2.   Stir in tomatoes with their liquid and, very gently, the okra. Cover and simmer for 15 to 20 minutes. Serve hot over *riz m'falfal* with Arabic bread.

Riz ou Loubiyeh

STRING BEANS WITH LAMB OVER RICE

◆

This recipe brings back wonderful childhood memories at our big family dinner table, everyone joking and telling stories, all at the same time: Mama and *Sitto* being sure we all had enough food. Serve over steamed rice or *riz m'falfal,* with Arabic bread and fresh cut vegetables.

2 pounds fresh green beans, julienne cut
1 pound lamb, cut in 1-inch cubes for stewing
2 tablespoons olive oil *or* clarified butter
2 onions, chopped
1/2 cup water
1 can whole tomatoes, chopped, with liquid
1 small can tomato sauce, plus one can of water
1/2 teaspoon salt
1/2 teaspoon black pepper
dash cinnamon
dash cayenne pepper

1.   Rinse and cut green beans.
2.   Sauté lamb in oil or butter for 5 minutes, then add onions and seasonings. Continue to stir and brown over medium heat 10 minutes.
3.   Add green beans, tomatoes with their liquid, tomato sauce, and water. Cover and simmer over low flame for 45 minutes, stirring occasionally. Taste and adjust seasoning. Serve over *riz m'falfal* with Arabic bread.

Sheikh al Mihshi

Stuffed Eggplant with Lamb and Pine Nuts

◆

The name translates to The Sheik of Stuffed Dishes, which says it all. It is a delicious, elegant creation baked and served over rice—a memorable meal. Similar to *batinjan mihshi*, this recipe is served over *riz m'falfal*, while the other has rice in the filling.

FILLING

> 1 1/2 pounds lamb, minced or coarsely ground (page 69)
> 1 large onion, finely chopped
> 1/4 cup pine nuts
> 2 tablespoons clarified butter *or* olive oil
> 1/2 teaspoon salt
> 1/4 teaspoon pepper
> 1/4 teaspoon cayenne
> 1/2 teaspoon cinnamon
> 1/2 teaspoon ground allspice
> 2 teaspoons lemon juice

ASSEMBLY

> 2 large eggplants or 12 Japanese (Arabic) eggplants
> 1/4 cup clarified butter, melted
> 2 cups sautéed lamb filling (above)
> 2 small cans tomato sauce
> 2 cans water
> 1/3 cup lemon juice
> 1/2 teaspoon salt
> 1/4 teaspoon pepper
> 1/4 teaspoon cayenne
> 1/2 teaspoon cinnamon
> 1/3 cup lemon juice

1. Sauté lamb until well done in clarified butter or equal parts butter and olive oil with finely chopped onion, salt and whole

Alice's Kitchen
Lamb

pine nuts. Season with pepper, cayenne, cinnamon, allspice and lemon juice just before cooking is complete, and set aside.

2.   Peel eggplants and season with salt and pepper. Set aside for a few minutes to drain. Pat eggplants dry, arrange them in a deep baking tray, and baste with clarified butter on all sides. Broil until light brown and tender, turning frequently for approximately 15 minutes.

3.   Cool eggplants and cut as follows:

Medium eggplants are quartered lengthwise.

Large ones are cut lengthwise first, in half, then in thirds, and finally into sixths, so you have elongated pieces. Cut a slit into the length, not all the way through—just deep enough to make a pocket, leaving 1/2"-1" uncut at each end.

If you use Japanese eggplants just make 1 cut into length of eggplant.

4.   Return them to baking tray and stuff with lamb filling. Pour tomato sauce over the filled eggplants and refill each can with water and pour into the tray. Season with salt, pepper, and cinnamon. Drizzle lemon juice over top and cover tray with foil.

5.   Bake at 375°F for 1 hour, until eggplant is tender and sauce has thickened. Serve over rice with sauce, *zoom,* from the baking tray and bread.

Batinjan Mihshi

STUFFED EGGPLANT WITH LAMB, TOMATO AND RICE

◆

Very similar to *Sheikh al Mihshi*, but with subtle differences—*sheikh al mihshi* is baked and *batinjan mihshi* is cooked on the stovetop. Small eggplants, 3-4 inches in length, are not peeled in this dish as in its counterpart recipe and the lamb is raw rather than sautéed before stuffing. Mother and *Sitto* prepared this exquisitely—it was a very special dish, when eggplants were in season. An excellent vegetarian version of this was prepared for me by my cousins in Lebanon, see recipe on page 135.

12 Japanese (Arabic) eggplants, rinsed unpeeled

FILLING

2 cups coarsely ground lamb
1/2 cup rice, rinsed and drained
1 small can tomato sauce, divided
1/3 cup lemon juice
1/8 teaspoon cinnamon
1/2 teaspoon salt
3/4 teaspoon black pepper
dash cayenne pepper
dash of allspice

FOR THE POT

several lamb bones
1 can whole tomatoes, chopped
1/3 cup lemon juice
3-4 black peppercorns

1.   Rinse and core eggplants as in *kousa mihshi* recipe page 102. Place them in salted water for about ten minutes and then drain them before stuffing.
2.   Parboil lamb bones for 15 minutes and arrange on the bottom of a deep pot. In the meantime, prepare the filling.

3.   In a bowl, mix lamb with rice, spices and half of the tomato sauce. Stuff eggplants with filling mixture about a half inch from the top. Arrange them on top of lamb bones in an upright position. Pour chopped tomatoes and remaining tomato sauce over eggplants with 2 cans of water. Season with a little more salt, pepper, and lemon juice over top. Cover and bring to boil.

4.   Turn down heat and simmer for an hour or so, until eggplant is tender and sauce has thickened. Serve drizzled with sauce, *zoom*, from the baking tray and Arabic bread, *khoobz*.

Malfouf Mihshi Bil Lahme ou Riz

CABBAGE ROLLS WITH LAMB AND RICE

◆

The lemony flavor and delicate texture of *malfouf mihshi* more than compensate for the aroma of cabbage as it cooks. Whole cabbage leaves contain the filling of rice and lamb. Serve with Arabic bread hot, warm, or cold and cut raw vegetables.

1 large head cabbage or 2 medium heads

STUFFING
1 pound coarsely ground lamb
3/4 cup rice, rinsed and drained
3/4 teaspoon salt
1/2 teaspoon black pepper
1/2 teaspoon cayenne pepper
1/2 teaspoon cinnamon
1/2 teaspoon allspice
1/3 cup lemon juice

FOR THE POT
several lamb bones, parboiled and rinsed (optional)
cabbage ribs and small leaves
1/2 cup lemon juice
10-12 small garlic cloves, unpeeled
5 black peppercorns

1.   Core cabbage by inserting knife point around the core from each side, towards the center of the cabbage.
2.   Blanch cabbage by placing the entire head in boiling water and removing leaves one at a time, until slightly tender, limp, and bright green in color, being careful not to overcook. Blanching removes their crispness so they can be easily rolled. As they separate from the head place leaves into a colander to cool and drain for stuffing. Set aside and make stuffing.

ALICE'S KITCHEN

LAMB

STUFFING & ASSEMBLY

1. Put rice, seasonings, and lemon juice in a bowl and mix thoroughly. Add lamb and mix well.

2. Open leaves flat on a clean, flat surface and cut main rib of cabbage leaf out. Outer leaves can be cut in half if they are very large and used to make two rolls. Line bottom of a deep pot with parboiled and rinsed lamb bones or with small cabbage leaves and the rib pieces.

3. One cabbage leaf at a time, spoon several teaspoons of stuffing across one end and roll closed, tucking sides and extra parts of leaf into the center. Stack rolls in deep pot on top of leaves and ribs. When you have one layer of rolls, distribute a few whole unpeeled garlic cloves over them and continue layering in rolls, adding garlic here and there.

4. Add water to almost cover cabbage rolls. Sprinkle a little salt, the lemon juice, and black peppercorns over the top. Place a dish over rolls to hold them intact and also cover pot with lid. Cook on high until boiling. Turn down and steam for about 30 minutes.

5. Remove dish and continue to simmer, covered, until water has been absorbed and meat is done, another 30 minutes. Let stand in covered pot for ten minutes or more before serving.

Kousa Mihshi

LEBANESE SQUASH STUFFED WITH LAMB AND RICE

◆

This was one of my favorite dishes, perhaps because I was allowed to help *Sitto* stuff the light green Lebanese squash harvested from our garden. *Sitto* even let me try to core it using one of the corers my mother had made from brass tubing. This was tricky for a 10-year-old, because it is easy to cut through the side or the bottom of the squash. Lebanese squash wasn't available in the grocery, so if we weren't raising any that year our Lebanese friends, the McKannas, shared their crop with us. Several U.S. seed companies now sell Lebanese zucchini seeds, but small yellow crooknecks or dark green zucchini can also be used. Squash corers are available at Middle Eastern import stores.

> 10 small green *or* yellow squash, about 4-6" long
> FILLING
> 1/2 cup rice
> 1/2 teaspoon cinnamon
> 4 whole allspice kernels, ground
>   *or* 1/2 teaspoon ground allspice
> 1/2 teaspoon salt
> 1/2 teaspoon black pepper
> 1/4 teaspoon cayenne pepper
> 1 tablespoon lemon juice
> 2 cups lamb, finely chopped or coarsely ground, page 69
> 1 small can tomato sauce, divided

ALICE'S KITCHEN

LAMB

FOR THE POT
  several lamb bones, parboiled and rinsed (optional)
  1 clove garlic
  tomato sauce
  1 large can whole tomatoes, coarsely chopped
  2 tablespoons lemon juice
  4 whole peppercorns
  3 1/2 cups water

1.   Rinse and drain rice and place in a bowl. Mix in seasonings, half the tomato sauce, a tablespoon of lemon juice, and the lamb.

2.   Parboil the lamb bones, rinse them, arrange them in the bottom of a deep pot and set aside. If unavailable, place a rack on the bottom of the pot upon which to set the squash.

3.   Cut off the tops of the squash and core them carefully so as not to crack them or pierce the bottom: Gently insert a corer and remove the first inch and a half of the core by rotating the corer clockwise with your right hand and the squash counter-clockwise with your left. As you turn, the marrow will be extruded. Ideally, there will be 1/8 inch thickness of squash around the hollow core. Save the seedy pulp for other dishes, such as *kousa ros* and *m'farkey b'kousa*. Place cored squash in a bowl of salted water flavored with a clove of garlic until all are cored.

4.   Take each cored squash, drain water from its center, and gently fill with lamb and rice mixture, being careful not to crack the shell, to about one-half inch from the top.

5.   Arrange stuffed squash upright in pot over the lamb bones. Pour in the remaining tomato sauce, the chopped tomatoes with their juice, the additional lemon juice, peppercorns and water. Cover pot, place on stovetop with heat on high until sauce begins to boil, then reduce heat to low and simmer approximately 1 hour until rice is done, squash is tender and sauce is thick.

6.   When serving, cut squash open and pour tomato sauce from the pot over them to the taste of the individual. Best with Arabic bread, carrot sticks, celery, cucumbers, romaine lettuce and other cut vegetables.

ALICE'S KITCHEN
LAMB

Waraq 'inab, Yabra, or Waraq Arish

STUFFED GRAPE LEAVES WITH LAMB AND RICE

◆

Grape leaves were such a precious commodity that a grapevine was planted in our backyard especially to meet our harvest needs. They were almost more important than the grapes, as no fruits came from this grapevine, just the young, tender, shiny leaves picked in a tidy stack, tiny stems pointing to the sky. They were taken directly into the kitchen to be filled with lamb and rice or vegetables and rice, then rolled into this famous dish, called *waraq 'inab, yabra,* or *waraq arish*.

Toward the end of the growing season, Mother tucked them into freezer bags and into the freezer for winter suppers when the vines were dormant. If you do not have fresh or frozen grape leaves, canned grape leaves are wilted and roll easily straight from the jar. If you pick your own, be sure they are unblemished, young, shiny and not fuzzy. Large leaves can be picked if they are still tender, and the variety that has a broad leaf will hold more filling, but small ones are wonderful for *mezza*.

40 fresh grape leaves *or* 1 quart canned or frozen leaves
FILLING
2 cups finely chopped lamb (page 69)
3/4 cup rice, rinsed and drained
1/2 teaspoon cinnamon
4 whole allspice kernels, ground
1/2 teaspoon salt
1/2 teaspoon black pepper
1/4 teaspoon cayenne pepper

FOR THE POT
1 pound lamb bones, parboiled and rinsed (optional)
4 cups water
1/3 cup lemon juice
5 black peppercorns

ALICE'S KITCHEN

LAMB

1.   Place rice in large bowl and mix in seasonings. Add lamb, mix well and set aside.

2.   Arrange parboiled lamb bones in a layer covering the bottom of a deep pot and set aside. If unavailable, use grape leaves to line the bottom of the pot.

3.   Blanch fresh or frozen grape leaves in warm water briefly to wilt. Lay one leaf out on board with veins facing up and place a teaspoon or two of stuffing across the width of the leaf, to equal the thickness of your index finger. Adjust the amount of filling to the scale of the grape leaf.

4.   Fold sides in and roll up. Place each rolled grape leaf into the pot on top of the bones, forming a row. Begin the next row perpendicular to it and continue stacking them in the pot in this manner, until you have used up all of the filling.

5.   Add lemon juice and water to almost cover grape leaves. Place a plate on tope of the grape leaves, top side down, to hold them intact and cover pot with lid. Cook over high heat until boiling, then reduce heat and simmer until water has been absorbed and rice is done, about an hour and a half. It is good to let them steam in the pot for fifteen minutes after cooking prior to serving.

6.   The traditional way to serve *waraq 'inab*, is to remove the plate, then flip the pot upside down on a larger platter, so the lamb bones on top form a visually interesting construction with grape leaves underneath. Serve with carrot sticks, celery, cucumbers, olives, *labne* and Arabic bread.

Ghamme ma Fattee

STUFFED LAMB TRIPE WITH DRESSING

◆

S*itto's ghamme,* stuffed tripe, recipe is an excellent example of using all parts of the lamb, creating dishes that Mother and her generation considered delicacies, but we squeamish kids didn't.

2 1/2 pounds lamb or beef tripe
salt and baking soda

FILLING

2 pounds lamb, finely chopped
1/2 cup long grain rice, rinsed and drained
1/4 teaspoon allspice
1/2 teaspoon black pepper
1/2 teaspoon cinnamon
1/2 teaspoon salt
2 tablespoons lemon juice
1 onion, finely chopped (optional)
1 can garbanzo beans, drained (optional)

FOR THE POT

5 peppercorns
1/2 teaspoon salt

FATTEE DRESSING

3 loaves Arabic bread, toasted to crisp light brown
5 cloves garlic
1/4 teaspoon salt
1 cup vinegar

1.   Place rice in a mixing bowl, add seasonings, and mix well. If you wish to use onion and garbanzo beans, mix them in. Add ground lamb, mix well and set aside.

2.   Sprinkle salt and baking soda liberally over tripe; rinse

it well and allow to drain. Tie one end of tripe with string to close it. Using a funnel, loosely stuff it with meat and rice filling, allowing room for rice to expand in cooking. Fill each section to whatever length it is, and then tie end closed with string.

3.   Puncture each length of stuffed tripe every 12 inches with a fork. Place in a deep pot and fill with water to cover the tripe. Add peppercorns and salt. Cover and bring to a boil. Reduce heat and simmer for an hour to an hour and a half. Test to see if it is done, by cutting a little section.

4.   While it is cooking, prepare *fattee*, bread dressing to serve over it. Toast bread until light brown and crispy. When cool, crush bread into half inch pieces. In a bowl, mash garlic into a paste with salt. Stir in vinegar. Place bread in a bowl and sprinkle with a few drops of broth from the *ghamme*. Pour vinegar/garlic mix over bread and toss well.

5.   Serve tripe cut into 4 inch sections topped with *fatte*. A Lebanese delicacy, to be sure.

Djej

◆

Chicken

Mama remembers eating chicken, *djej*, for dinner or *ghadda*, the main meal of the day in Douma on Sundays. *Sitto* butchered the chicken and then washed it well with baking soda and salt, after cutting it up into sections. The recipes here are the ones Mother and *Sitto* made most frequently when we were growing up in Los Angeles that we love the most.

Djej Mihshi

STUFFED CHICKEN WITH LAMB AND RICE

In the village, every family raised their own chickens because they efficiently consumed kitchen food scraps and consistently converted them into eggs. Chickens were also the special dish for Sunday dinner. To carry on the village tradition in our affluent Los Angeles neighborhood during the 1950s, we risked disregarding prevailing conventions and kept chickens—briefly, anyway, until the rooster's cock-a-doodle-doo became too disonant and the neighbors complained. Here is our authentic Lebanese recipe for special occasion stuffed chicken. Mother and *Sitto* made two types of rice for chicken—one that was stuffed inside the chicken and a slightly different version that is cooked on the side to provide enough for extra guests. Recipe for the additional rice is on the following page.

LAMB STUFFING

    2 cups lamb, minced or coarsely ground

    1/2 cup rice, rinsed

    1/2 teaspoon cinnamon

    1/4 teaspoon allspice

    1/2 teaspoon salt

    1/2 teaspoon black pepper

    1/4 teaspoon cayenne pepper

FOR THE POT

    1/8 cup olive oil

    3 cups water

    5 peppercorns

    1.   Mix above stuffing ingredients together well. Preheat oven to 350°F.

    2.   Rub chicken with salt and baking soda, to cleanse and remove pungency; rinse well. Stuff chicken with lamb and rice mixture. Close with small skewers, place in a roaster and rub with olive oil, salt and pepper. Add water and peppercorns; cover pot.

3. Bake approximately 1-1 1/2 hours, depending upon the size of the chicken. Test for doneness: a fork will easily pierce the leg when the chicken is done. Remove from oven and place stuffing in a platter along side cut piece of roasted chicken. Serve with Arabic bread, additional rice and *laban*.

SIDE DISH RICE

    1/2 pound ground lamb *or* finely chopped lamb
    2 tablespoons clarified butter
    1/4 cup pine nuts
    1/2 teaspoon salt
    1/2 teaspoon black pepper
    1/2 teaspoon allspice
    1/4 teaspoon cinnamon
    2 cups chicken broth
    1 cup rice, rinsed and drained

GARNISH

    1/2-1 cup blanched, slivered almonds *and/or* pine nuts

    Brown nuts in butter. Set aside to garnish rice before serving.

1. Sauté lamb in clarified butter. Add pine nuts and brown. Stir in seasonings. Add chicken broth, cover and bring to a boil.

2. Add rice, cover and steam 20 minutes, if using white rice, or 40 minutes if using brown rice. When rice is done, stir with fork, cover, and let stand for ten minutes before serving. Serve with chicken pieces; garnish with browned almonds or pine nuts. Scrumptious!

Sh'ariyeh ou Riz ma Djej

ORZO WITH RICE AND CHICKEN

◆

The very flavor and texture of this dish made it one of my top ten favorites. Chicken, rice, orzo, *laban* and bread...it is a great combination. Moist chicken and rice with tangy yogurt. Mmmm.

1 1/4 cups rice, rinsed or soaked, and drained
1 cup *sh'ariyeh* (a type of pasta known as rosa marina
    or orzo)
3 tablespoons clarified butter
6 pieces of chicken *or* 1 whole chicken, cut up
2 whole allspice kernels
3 cinnamon sticks
1 bay leaf
3 whole black peppercorns
1/2 teaspoon salt

1. If chicken is whole, cut it into six pieces. Rub chicken with salt and baking soda. Rinse well in cold water. Place in a deep pot with water to cover. Add cinnamon sticks, bay leaf, allspice, peppercorns, and salt. Bring to a boil and skim top, removing and discarding any residue that forms. Turn down heat and simmer until tender, about 1/2 hour. Remove chicken from heat and set aside.

2. In a deep pot over medium heat, melt butter and add *sh'ariyeh* to it. Stir and brown it for about 10 minutes. Add rice; continue browning and stirring for 3 minutes.

3. Remove chicken from broth and wrap in foil to keep warm. Strain hot chicken broth (about 3 1/2 cups) over rice and stir. Cover pot and cook over high heat for about 10 minutes until boiling. Lower heat and simmer for 15 minutes more and turn off heat. Let stand for 15 minutes.

4. Stir with fork and taste and adjust seasonings. Serve chicken on top of rice with yogurt, *laban*. Serve with cut radishes, carrots, lettuce and Arabic bread.

Djej Mishwi

BARBEQUED CHICKEN WITH GARLIC MARINADE

◆

1 whole chicken cut into parts
    or 8 pieces of breast, thigh, drumstick and wings
7 cloves garlic
1/2 teaspoon salt
1 cup lemon juice
1/8 cup olive oil
1/2 teaspoon black pepper
1/4 teaspoon cayenne pepper

1.   Skin chicken, if desired, then rinse chicken pieces with water, and rub them with baking soda and salt. Rinse well with water, drain and place in a bowl.

2.   In a small bowl, mash garlic into a paste with salt. Add lemon juice and pepper. Pour into bowl with chicken pieces, toss so that pieces are completely coated with marinade. Cover bowl and refrigerate for 2 hours.

3.   Barbeque chicken on hot grill for 7 minutes on each side until golden brown or as you like. Serve with *toum ou zeit*, garlic mayonnaise, *salata*, and french fried potatoes—a summer favorite.

Djej M'hammar
BROILED CHICKEN WITH GARLIC MARINADE
◆

1 whole chicken, cut up
    or 8 pieces of breast, thigh, drumstick and wings
7 cloves garlic
1/4 teaspoon salt
1/4 teaspoon citric acid
1/2 cup lemon juice
1/2 teaspoon sugar
1/2 teaspoon black pepper
1/4 teaspoon cayenne pepper
1/8 teaspoon cinnamon
1/8 teaspoon allspice
1/2 teaspoon steero granules
1/2 cup mayonnaise
1/4 cup olive oil
1 teaspoon paprika

1.   Rinse chicken with water, then rub with baking soda and salt. Rinse well with water and drain.

2.   In a large bowl, mash garlic into a paste using a little salt and citric acid. Add lemon juice, spices, mayonnaise and olive oil and mix well. Add chicken pieces to marinate, coating each piece thoroughly, cover and refrigerate.

3.   Preheat oven on to broil. Put chicken pieces in a roasting pan and place under broiler to brown for 7 minutes. Sprinkle with paprika. Turn to other side, add paprika and brown the other side.

4.   Sprinkle with water, cover with foil, reduce heat to 325°F and bake for 5 minutes more. Serve with baked or french fried potatoes.

Riz bit feen

Upside down rice

◆

3 yellow onions, julienne cut
1 can garbanzo beans, drained
2 lamb shanks *or* 4 chicken pieces
2 tablespoons clarified butter or olive oil
1 cup rice, rinsed and drained
1/2 teaspoon salt
3 whole peppercorns
1/4 teaspoon ground allspice
4 cinnamon sticks

1. Rub chicken with baking soda and salt or rinse lamb shanks. Rinse well, drain and place in large pot. Cover with water, add seasonings and bring to a boil. Simmer 20 minutes. Let cool. Strain and reserve broth.

2. Sauté onions in clarified butter or olive oil in a deep pot until they are translucent. Add garbanzo beans and continue to sauté about 5 minutes.

3. Remove meat from bone and layer pieces over onions and beans. Stir in a little more salt, pepper, allspice and ground cinnamon. Add broth to cover the chicken or lamb. Add rice on top without stirring. Cover and bring to a boil, then reduce heat to low and simmer until rice is done, about 30 minutes.

4. Let stand for 10 minutes and then loosen rice from edges of pot. Place round platter on top of pot and flip over. Serve with bread, *laban*, and fresh cut vegetables. Appetizing and delicious.

Samak

◆

Fish

Since Douma is a high mountain village, in Mama's days there in the early 1920s, it was a long journey to the Mediterranean, even though its waters were clearly visible from the town's 3000 foot elevation. Because of the distance and the lack of good refrigeration, fish was not a frequent part of our family repertoire. In Los Angeles, fish remained a minor part of our diet. The exception was canned tuna fish for Fridays and Lent, which was lavished with lemon juice, as we preferred all of our fish dishes. Though few in number, these zesty fish recipes are delectable.

Samak Bil Furn Ma Taratour

BAKED FISH WITH TAHINI

◆

1 whole fish, 12-14"
olive oil
1/4 teaspoon salt
1/4 teaspoon pepper
1 large onion, finely chopped
1/3 cup lemon juice

FOR GARNISH
taratour sauce (page 37)
1/2 cup parsley sprigs
2 lemons, cut into wedges
1/2 cup sautéed pine nuts, *snobar*

1. Preheat oven to 350°F. Rinse fish, pat dry and rub with olive oil, salt and pepper. Wrap tightly in brown paper and place on baking tray. Bake for approximately a half hour, depending upon the thickness of the fish.

2. Meanwhile, sauté onion in olive oil for about 15 minutes. Set aside. Make *taratour* sauce and sauté pine nuts for garnish.

3. Remove and discard the paper, skin and bones of the fish. Arrange pieces of fish on a platter. Spread sautéed onion over the top. Drizzle with *taratour* sauce and lemon juice. Garnish with parsley, lemon wedges or slices and sautéed pine nuts.

Kibbe Bi Samak

FISH WITH BULGAR AND PINE NUT FILLING

◆

2 1/2 pound halibut filet
3 onions, quartered
3 cups #1 bulgar, rinsed and drained
1/2 teaspoon salt
1/2 teaspoon pepper
2 tablespoons orange zest
1/2 cup ice water

FILLING

3 onions, julienne cut
1/2 cup *snobar*, pine nuts
1/4 teaspoon salt
3/4 cup olive oil

1. Remove skin and bone from fish and rinse. Preheat oven to 425°F.
2. Grind fish with bulgar and quartered onions in food grinder or processor. Mix in seasonings, and grind again mixing with ice water.
3. Sauté julienne cut onions, salt, and pine nuts in all of the olive oil until light brown. Lift nuts and onions from pan with slotted spoon and reserve oil.
4. Lightly oil an 8 x 13 inch baking tray and layer half of the ground fish mixture into tray, approximately 1/2 inch thick. Spread filling evenly across bottom layer and then spread remaining *kibbe* to cover, smoothing out the surface with your hand dipped in ice water.
5. Pour olive oil from sauté evenly over the top of the *kibbe*. Bake for fifteen minutes in lower oven rack. Cut and serve hot or cold with *salata*.

Samak Miqli Ma Taratour

FRIED FISH WITH TAHINI SAUCE

◆

1/4 cup olive oil
halibut or rock bass filets
salt and pepper
1/2 cup flour
1/4 cup lemon juice
3/4 cup *taratour* sauce (page 37)

1.   Rinse fish filets in water and pat dry. Season with salt and pepper and then lay them in a plate on top of flour to coat each side. Heat olive oil in a skillet and lay fish filets in skillet.

2.   Fry for about 5 minutes on each side until golden brown, but still tender. Remove from heat and drain on a paper towel. Serve on a platter drizzled with lemon juice and *taratour* sauce.

Ros Samak

FISH PATTIES

1 1/2 pound fish, rinsed, skinned, and boned
2 potatoes, boiled
2 onions, quartered
1 egg, separated
1/2 teaspoon salt
1/2 teaspoon black pepper
1/4 teaspoon cinnamon
1/2 teaspoon cumin
1 teaspoon vinegar
1/2 cup flour
1 cup bread crumbs
1 cup olive or vegetable oil, for frying
3/4 cup *taratour* sauce (page 37)
2 lemons, cut into wedges for garnish

1.   Grind fish together with potatoes in food grinder two times. Place in a bowl and add egg yolk, seasonings, and vinegar. Mix well. Stir egg white in a flat bowl. Place flour into a flat plate.

2.   Form fish into patties or rounds and dip into flour first, then into egg white and then bread crumbs.

3.   Heat oil in skillet and fry patties on each side until light brown. Remove from skillet and drain on paper towel. Serve hot or at room temperature with *taratour* sauce, lemon wedges and *salata*.

Samak Mishwi

BROILED OR GRILLED FISH WITH TAHINI SAUCE

◆

halibut or rock bass filets
salt and pepper
3 cloves garlic, minced
1/2 cup lemon juice
1/2 cup *taratour* sauce (page 37)
2 lemons, cut into wedges for garnish

1.   Heat oven to broil or grill. Rinse fish in water and pat dry. Rub with olive oil and season lightly with salt and pepper. Lay filets in a broiling pan and sprinkle with minced garlic and lemon juice.

2.   Broil for about 5 minutes on each side until just golden brown, and still tender. Remove from heat and serve on a platter with lemon wedges and *taratour* sauce.

Siyeme

◆

Vegetarian entrees

M'jaddrah

Lentils and Rice with Caramelized Onions

◆

This is a favorite from childhood, when my gardening passions were budding and I used to pretend that the brown *m'jaddrah* was the earth and the green salad on top of it, the vegetables I was growing. The combination is delicious with bread and provides complementary proteins. Caramelized onions lacing the top elevate this simple, nutritious food to gourmet status. Best with *salata* and scooped up with Arabic bread.

1 cup onions, chopped to sauté
1/8 cup olive oil
1/2 cup brown or white rice
1 cup lentils
3 onions, julienne cut, to caramelize
4 cups water
1/2 teaspoon salt
1/4 teaspoon cayenne pepper

1. Sauté chopped onions in olive oil until slightly brown.
2. Meanwhile, rinse lentils and rice. If you use brown rice, add both lentils and rice to onions and sauté a few minutes more. Add water, salt, and cayenne. Cover, bring to a boil and simmer for 1 1/2 hours. If you use white rice, add it to the pot after the other ingredients have simmered for nearly an hour.
3. Stir from time to time and add water if necessary: *m'jaddrah* can be made as dry as rice or as wet as a thick porridge. While the lentils and rice simmer, julienne cut three onions and sauté them in olive oil, first on high heat, stirring constantly, then on low, until they are golden brown.
4. Let *m'jaddrah* stand for 15 minutes after it is done before putting it onto a serving platter. Delicious hot, at room temperature or cold, heaped on a platter with the caramelized onions lacing the top.

M'jaddrah ma Burghul

LENTILS AND BULGAR

Made with bulgar instead of rice, this variation on *m'jaddrah* has a hearty, wheat flavor.

1/8 cup olive oil
1/2 cup bulgar, rinsed
1 cup lentils, rinsed
1 cup chopped onions
3 onions, julienne cut, to caramelized
4 cups water
1/2 teaspoon salt
1/4 teaspoon cayenne

1. Sauté chopped onions in olive oil until slightly brown.
2. Add lentils, water, salt, and cayenne to onions. Cover, bring to a boil and simmer for an hour.
3. Stir in bulgar, check water level and add water if needed; continue to simmer for twenty minutes, or until done.
4. In the meantime, julienne cut three onions and slowly sauté in olive oil until golden brown. Serve *m'jaddrah* on a platter with caramelized onions lacing the top, with *salata* and Arabic bread. May be eaten hot, at room temperature or cold.

M'dardarah

LENTILS AND RICE

◆

And yet another variation on *m'jaddrah*, this one has more rice to lentils than *m'jaddrah* and a drier consistency—more like steamed rice. Quite delicious, as are the other variations, *m'dardarah* is also served with *salata* and Arabic bread and of course the delicious carmelized onions. Serve hot, at room temperature or cold in the summer.

1/8 cup olive oil
1/2 cup brown (or white) rice
1/2 cup lentils
1 cup chopped onions
3 onions, julienne cut, to caramelize
3 cups water
1/2 teaspoon salt
1/4 teaspoon cayenne

1. Sauté chopped onions in olive oil until slightly brown.
2. Meanwhile, rinse lentils and rice. If you use brown rice, add both lentils and rice to onions and sauté a few minutes more. Add water, salt, and cayenne. Cover, bring to a boil and simmer for 1 1/2 hours. If you use white rice, add it to the pot after the other ingredients have simmered for nearly an hour.
3. Check water level and stir about midway, adding water if needed so that it does not stick.
4. In the meantime, julienne cut three onions and slowly sauté in olive oil until golden brown. When *m'dardarah* is done, let it stand for 10 minutes before transferring it to a serving platter. Scatter the caramelized onions over the top and enjoy.

Riz ou Kousa

RICE AND SQUASH

Sitto made this excellent summer dish when squash, *kousa*, were abundant. Simple to prepare and tasty, it is one of the first dishes I was able to cook on my own. Let your ten year old try it with your guidance! It makes a great summer potluck dish, served hot, at room temperature or cold scooped in Arabic bread with fresh cut vegetables along side.

1 onion, finely chopped
1/4 cup olive oil
5 yellow squash or small zucchini, chopped into 1" cubes
3 stalks celery (optional)
3/4 cup rice, rinsed
3 fresh tomatoes, chopped, plus 1/2 cup water
    or 1 large can whole tomatoes, chopped, with juice
    or 1/2 small can tomato sauce, plus 1 cup water
1/2 teaspoon salt
1/4 teaspoon black pepper
dash cayenne pepper

1. In a deep pot, sauté onion in olive oil for 10 minutes and then add squash, celery, and tomato. Sauté 10 minutes. Add rice and water. Cover and bring to boil, then reduce heat and simmer for a half hour or until rice is done. Brown rice takes twice as long as white rice.

2. Stir occasionally and check to see if more water is needed. Let stand in pot for ten minutes before serving. Present on a colorful platter with Arabic bread.

Burghul ou Kousa

BULGAR AND SQUASH

◆

In this variation on *riz ou kousa* using bulgar, the wonderful flavor of wheat comes through as well as its nutty texture. Serve with Arabic bread and fresh cut vegetables.

1/4 cup olive oil
2 onions, chopped
2 celery stalks, chopped
4 yellow squash or small zucchini, chopped into 1"cubes
3/4 cup *burghul,* bulgar, rinsed
3 fresh tomatoes, chopped, plus 1/2 cup water
    or 1 large can whole tomatoes, with liquid
    or 1/2 small can tomato sauce, plus 1 cup water
1/2 teaspoon salt
1/4 teaspoon black pepper
1/4 teaspoon cayenne pepper
dash cinnamon

1.   In a deep pot, sauté onion in olive oil for 10 minutes and then add celery, squash and chopped tomato. Sauté 10 minutes.

2.   Add bulgar, water and seasonings. Cover and bring to boil, then reduce heat and simmer for a half hour, until bulgar is done. Stir occasionally and check to see if more water is needed. Let stand in pot for ten minutes before serving.

M'farkey b'kousa

SQUASH STEW

Stews are typical of the one-pot meals essential to our cuisine. Quick to prepare, served over rice, eaten with Arabic bread, this particular one is nutritious, tasty and satisfying, using the cores or squash marrow from *kousa mihshi*. Serve over rice with Arabic bread and fresh cut vegetables.

1/8 cup olive oil
1 onion, minced
1 clove garlic
1 large can whole tomatoes, chopped
    or 3 chopped fresh tomatoes with their juice
3 cups yellow or green squash marrow from cored
    zucchini *or* finely chopped squash
1/2 teaspoon salt
1/4 teaspoon black pepper
1/4 teaspoon cayenne pepper
1/4 teaspoon cinnamon

1.   Sauté onion and garlic in olive oil over medium heat in a pan. When onion is transparent, stir in whole tomatoes.

2.   If using squash marrow, squeeze out and set aside liquid for use in soup stock. Stir squash and seasonings in with onions and tomatoes. Cover and simmer until squash is done, about twenty-five minutes.

Fatayir b'spanegh

SPINACH PIES

◆

Better tasting after they have cooled from the oven, spinach pies were difficult to get enough of when Mother and *Sitto* baked them. As a child, I loved trying to make these and am grateful to Mother and *Sitto* for this early opportunity to develop a skill and love for making them. They are even more fun to make when there are two or three people involved in the production, chatting and pinching; the time making these labor-intensive delicacies flies. They are very similar to making meat pies, except spinach pie triangles are totally closed. Below are alternate ideas if you don't have time to make small pies. Feta cheese crumbled into the filling is a delicious variation. First prepare the dough following the basic bread dough recipe on page 162 and while it rises, the filling can be made.

DOUGH
follow recipe for basic bread dough

FILLING
2 bunches of spinach, rinsed and dried
    or 1 package of frozen spinach
1 bunch parsley, rinsed, stemmed
2 cups fresh spearmint, rinsed and stemmed
1 bunch green onions
2 small white onions
1/2 cup celery tops
2 small zucchini, grated (optional)
1/2 teaspoon salt
1/2 tablespoon pepper
1/2 teaspoon cayenne
1/4 teaspoon citric acid
    or 1/3 cup lemon juice
2 tablespoons olive oil

FILLING
1. Chop onions and put in large bowl. Stir in salt, pepper and cayenne.
2. Finely chop spinach, parsley, mint, celery tops, grated zucchini and mix in thoroughly. Add citric acid or lemon juice and oil just before filling dough. Taste and adjust seasoning.

ASSEMBLY
1. Using a rolling pin, roll out one ball of dough on a well-floured surface to about 1/8" thickness.
2. Use a mason jar cap (3 1/2" diameter), to cut out as many circles as possible, and put scraps of dough into a bowl and set aside.
3. Place two tablespoons of filling into a circle and close it into a triangle as explained on page 82 for meat pies, with one difference—the dough on spinach pies is pinched totally closed.

SUGGESTIONS ON FORMING TRIANGLES FILLED WITH SPINACH
Keep fingers dry and floured while pinching dough so it will stay closed and keep spinach filling out of the joint. Add a tablespoon of wheat germ or flour to filling if too much liquid accumulates in bowl. Fill pie as much as possible because spinach shrinks with cooking. Push in the point of the triangle before pinching closed; this keeps juices from escaping while it bakes.

4. Place pies on oiled baking tray or tray lined with baking parchment about 1/4 inch apart. Preheat oven to 375°F.
5. Knead dough scraps and form into a ball, dust with flour, cover and let rise again. If you have extra dough and no more filling, use it to make *tilme b'zaa'tar*, plain *tilme, khoobz,* or a pizza! Another option is to freeze extra dough for later use: just roll it into a ball, then dust with flour, cover tightly with plastic wrap and freeze in a plastic freezer bag.
6. Bake on lowest oven rack until bottoms are golden brown, about 10 to 12 minutes. Move tray to top rack until tops are lightly browned, another 10 minutes.
7. Remove from trays and drain on opened paper bags to absorb oil and cool.

To FREEZE PIES FOR LATER BAKING

Place unbaked pies on ungreased tray in freezer for several hours until individually frozen and then pack in freezer bags to store for a month or so. Or freeze baked pies for reheating prior to serving.

VARIATIONS

• Make dough ahead and freeze, by wrapping orange-sized balls tightly in plastic and placing in a freezer bag. Remove from freezer a few hours before and place on counter to thaw and rise.

• Instead of small circles of dough, form pastry into 6 to 8 inch circles of dough thus, having fewer large triangles—the type available in restaurants because they are quicker to make. In Lebanon, these are served with a lemon squeezed over the top or *zaa'tar* sprinkled on to add a bit of zest.

• A Syrian friend of mine, *Sitt* Amine, forms her spinach pies as one large rolled-out piece of dough, places it on a baking tray, and puts spinach filling an inch thick covering one half of the dough round to 1/2 inch from the edge. She folds the other half of the dough across to cover the filling, rolls over it lightly with the rolling pin and then bakes it as one big piece, with a little olive oil brushed across the top. Cool and cut into small, easy to hold sections after baking.

• Precook fresh spinach filling in a sauté pan before stuffing to reduce the moisture content and compact it.

• Add 1/2 pound crumbled feta cheese to spinach filling.

'Ijhee

OMELETTE WITH PARSLEY, MINT, & ONION

◆

A tasty frittata-like omelette, *'ihjee*, is light, delicious and simple to make. In the coldest of Oregon winters, I find parsley and mint in my garden for this superb dish. It can be served for breakfast, brunch, lunch or dinner, tucked into a round of pocket bread— with more bread, feta cheese or *jibn*, olives, sliced cucumbers, and fig jam served along side.

1 small white onion, finely chopped
1/2 teaspoon salt
1/4 teaspoon black pepper
dash cayenne pepper
1/2 teaspoon cinnamon
2 tablespoons flour
1 teaspoon baking powder
4 green onions, finely chopped
1/2 bunch parsley, finely chopped
4 eggs
1/4 cup clarified butter and oil, equal parts
1/4 cup fresh spearmint, finely chopped (optional)
1/2 cup celery tops, finely chopped (optional)
1/4 cup grated zucchini (optional)

1.   Place white onions in bowl and stir in spices, flour and baking powder.

2.　Mix in green onions, parsley and, if desired, mint, celery and zucchini. Crack eggs over the top and mix well with a fork.

3.　Heat butter and oil in skillet to medium high. Pour in mixture and spread it out evenly. Cook until golden brown and top is not runny, about 5 to 10 minutes. Flip over carefully and brown other side.

A SIMPLE WAY TO FLIP *'IJHEE:*

Place a dish over the skillet that extends beyond the edge; using pot holders, hold the plate flat onto the skillet and briskly turn the skillet upside down transferring the omelette onto the plate. Then slide the omelette off the plate back into the skillet to brown other side. Serve hot, warm or cold inside pocket bread.

Kousa Mihshi Siyeme

SQUASH STUFFED WITH RICE

◆

Our vegetarian alternative to *kousa mihshi* stuffed with rice, garbanzo beans, parsley and tomato is satisfying and wonderfully seasoned. If light green Lebanese squash are unavailable, use small yellow crooknecks or dark green zucchini. This wonderful dish can be made with or without garbanzo beans; mint is also an optional ingredient.

10 small lebanese squash, *kousa*

FILLING

1 cup canned garbanzo beans, drained
   or 1/2 cup dry garbanzo beans, soaked overnight
1 cup rice, rinsed and drained
2 bunches parsley, finely chopped
1 bunch mint, finely chopped (optional)
1 bunch green onions, finely chopped
2 stalks celery with tops, diced
1/2 teaspoon salt
1/2 teaspoon black pepper
1/4 teaspoon cayenne pepper
1 can whole tomatoes, chopped
   or 1 pound fresh tomatoes
1 can tomato sauce
1/4 cup lemon juice

1. If using dry garbanzo beans, soak overnight. Drain water and add fresh water to cover. Cover pot, bring to a boil, then simmer for about 20 minutes. Cool, drain and remove skins from beans.

2. In a bowl, mix together rice, beans, seasonings and chopped greens.

3. Core squash according to directions on page 103. Fill

with rice mixture to 1/2 inch from top and arrange stuffed squash upright in a pot, propped against one another.

4.   Cover with whole tomatoes with their liquid, a little olive oil, lemon juice and one cup water. Cover and bring to boil over high heat on the stovetop, then lower heat and simmer approximately 45 minutes, until rice is done, squash is tender and sauce, *zoom*, is thick.

5.   Split each kousa in half on individual plates and pour on a little sauce. Serve hot with Arabic bread and fresh cut vegetables.

Batinjan Mihshi Siyeme

STUFFED EGGPLANT WITH RICE, TOMATO, AND PARSLEY

◆

Made for me by cousins in Lebanon, this vegetarian version of *batinjan mihshi* is truly excellent! Small eggplants, 3 to 4 inches in length, are stuffed as in *kousa mihshi,* stuffed squash.

12 small Japanese (Arabic) eggplants, rinsed, unpeeled

FILLING

1/2 cup rice, rinsed and drained

3 tomatoes, chopped

1 bunch green onions *or* 1 Spanish onion, finely chopped

1/2 bunch parsley, finely chopped

1/2 bunch mint, finely chopped

1/3 cup lemon juice

1/2 teaspoon salt

1/4 teaspoon pepper

1/4 teaspoon cayenne

FOR THE POT

1 small can tomato sauce

1/4 cup olive oil

1/3 cup lemon juice

1. Rinse and core eggplants as in *kousa mihshi* recipe, page 103. Place them in salted water for 10 minutes and then drain.

2. In a bowl, mix together rice, vegetables, lemon juice and spices. Taste and adjust seasoning.

3. Fill each eggplant with rice mixture to 1/2" from top and arrange upright in a deep pot, propped against one another.

4. Pour tomato sauce over them plus 2 cups of water, olive oil, and lemon juice. Cover and bring to boil. Turn down heat and simmer for an hour or so, until eggplant is tender and sauce has thickened.

5. Serve with sauce, *zoom,* and *khoobz.*

Malfouf mihshi siyeme

VEGETARIAN STUFFED CABBAGE ROLLS

◆

1 large or 2 medium heads cabbage

FILLING

1 bunch parsley
1/2 bunch mint
3 green onions
1 Spanish onion
3/4 cup garbanzo beans, soaked overnight,
    halved and skins removed
1/2 cup rice, rinsed and drained
1/2 head of celery, tops and stalks
1/2 teaspoon salt
1/4 teaspoon pepper
1/4 teaspoon cayenne
1/4 cup lemon juice
1/8 cup olive oil

FOR THE POT

10-12 small cloves of garlic, unpeeled
2 cups water
1/4 cup olive oil
1/3 cup lemon juice
salt

1.   Core cabbage by inserting knife point around the core from each side, toward the center of the cabbage.
2.   Blanch whole cabbage by placing in boiling water until slightly tender, limp and bright green in color. Separate leaves one at a time, as they wilt, and place in a colander. Set aside to cool and drain for stuffing. They just need to be flexible enough to roll.
3.   In bowl, mix rice, garbanzo beans, salt, pepper, lemon juice, and olive oil.

4.   Finely chop parsley, mint, onions and celery; mix them into rice mixture. Taste and adjust seasoning.

5.   Open cabbage leaves flat on a clean, flat surface and cut main rib out. Outer leaves can be cut in half if they are very large and used to make two rolls. Line bottom of a deep pot with small leaves and rib pieces.

6.   One cabbage leaf at a time, spoon several teaspoons of stuffing across one end and roll closed, tucking sides and extra parts of leaf into the center. Stack rolls in pot on top of leaves and ribs. When you have one layer of rolls, distribute whole unpeeled garlic cloves over them and continue layering in rolls and garlic.

7.   Pour water, a little salt, lemon juice and olive oil over the top. Place a plate upside down over rolls to hold them intact and cover pot with lid. Cook on high until boiling, then turn down heat and steam until rice is done, about an hour. Remove plate after cooked half way, about 30 minutes. Let stand for 15 minutes before serving.

Waraq 'Inab

Vegetarian Stuffed Grape Leaves

◆

Rolled grape leaves, either with meat and rice or rice and vegetables are one of the finest of Lebanese dishes. Please see recipe on page 104 about picking fresh grape leaves. Fresh chard leaves are a perfect substitute for grape leaves in this nutritious and delectable vegetarian composition.

40 fresh grape leaves *or* 1 quart canned or frozen leaves

FILLING
> 1 cup rice, rinsed
> 1 bunch green onions *or* 1 Spanish onion, finely chopped
> 1 bunch parsley, finely chopped
> 1/2 bunch mint, finely chopped
> 1 cup tomatoes, finely chopped
> 1/2 cup chick peas, precooked or canned (optional)
> 1/2 teaspoon salt
> 1/2 teaspoon black pepper
> 1/4 teaspoon cayenne pepper
> 1/4 cup lemon juice
> 1/8 cup olive oil

FOR THE POT
> 1/2 cup lemon juice
> 3 cups water
> 4 cloves garlic
> 1/8 cup olive oil

1.   In a large bowl, add seasonings to rice and mix well; add lemon juice and olive oil. Mix in chopped vegetables and chick peas. Taste and adjust seasoning.

2.   Place some grape leaves on the bottom of a deep pot and set aside. Blanch fresh or frozen grape leaves in warm water

to wilt. Canned grape leaves are wilted enough to roll easily.

3.   Lay one leaf out on board with veins facing up and place stuffing about the thickness of your index finger across the width of the leaf. Fold sides in and roll up.

4.   Place each rolled grape leaf into the pot forming a row, side by side. Begin the next row perpendicular to it and continue stacking them in the pot in this manner, until you have used up all of the filling. Nestle in garlic cloves between the rolls.

5.   Pour water, lemon juice and olive oil over them and place a plate on top of the grape leaves, top side down. Cook over high heat until boiling, then simmer until rice is done, approximately 45 minutes. Let stand for about 15 minutes before serving.

6.   Serve with carrot sticks, celery, cucumbers, olives, *labne* and Arabic bread.

Masbit il Darwish

EGGPLANT POTATO STEW

◆

Here is the original Lenten version of Monk's Rosary that our family ate and loved. Simple, hearty and nutritious as so many of our one-pot dishes are, this stew can be served on its own or over steamed rice or *riz m'falfal* with bread.

1 onion, julienne cut
2 potatoes, diagonal cubes or wedges
2 garlic cloves, chopped
4 zucchini or yellow squash, cut on diagonal
1 eggplant, cut into large cubes
1 can garbanzo beans, drained
1 can whole tomatoes
    or 4 fresh tomatoes, peeled, chopped, with juice
1/2 teaspoon salt
1/4 teaspoon cayenne pepper
1/4 cup olive oil

1.   Preheat oven to 350°F. Layer the above ingredients into a stew pot in the order presented above. Cover and bake for 30 minutes.

2.   Stir and continue to bake uncovered until liquid is absorbed, approximately 15 minutes more. Serve hot with Arabic bread and fresh cut vegetables.

Masbit il Darwish

MONK'S ROSARY

◆

The name of this implies that it is a poor person's food because it is meatless and in the past, eating meat was a sign of wealth. Times have changed with many people choosing a vegetarian diet. This is Mother's newer version of this stew with more vegetables than the one opposite, served on its own or over steamed rice or *riz m'falfal* with bread. This recipe makes a large pot, enough to feed a family.

    1 eggplant, cut into large cubes
    1 cup celery, diced
    2 potatoes, diced
    3 carrots, cut on diagonal
    1 can garbanzo beans, drained
    3 zucchini or yellow squash, cut on diagonal
    2 green or red peppers, cut into 1 inch chunks
    5 garlic cloves, chopped
    3 onions, julienne cut
    1 can whole tomatoes
        or 4 fresh tomatoes, peeled and chopped, with juice
    5 peppercorns
    1/2 teaspoon salt
    1/4 teaspoon cayenne pepper
    1/4 teaspoon cinnamon
    1/2 cup olive oil

1.   Preheat oven to 350°F. Layer the above ingredients into a stew pot in the order presented above. Cover and bake for an hour.

2.   Stir and continue to bake uncovered until sauce thickens, approximately 10 minutes more. Serve hot with Arabic bread and fresh cut vegetables.

Riz ou Fassoulia Siyeme

LIMA BEANS OR WHITE BEANS WITH TOMATO, OVER RICE

◆

H ere I have adapted a dish made traditionally with small bits of lamb into a vegetarian version. The rice and beans, *riz ou fassoulia*, are complementary proteins seasoned with the same spices as the lamb version and just as wonderful! Serve over steamed rice or *riz m'falfal* with fresh cut vegetables and Arabic bread.

> 2 tablespoons olive oil
> 2 medium onions, chopped
> 3 cloves garlic, chopped
> 1/2 teaspoon salt
> 3/4 teaspoon black pepper
> 1/4 teaspoon cayenne pepper
> 1/2 teaspoon cinnamon
> 1 can whole tomatoes, chopped, with liquid
> 2 packages frozen lima beans
> > *or* 3/4 cup dry navy beans, soaked overnight
> > plus 2 cups water

1.   In a deep pot, sauté onions, garlic and seasonings in olive oil over medium heat for about 15 minutes, stirring frequently.
2.   Add tomatoes, with their liquid and the beans. Turn heat up, cover pot and bring to a boil. Then reduce heat to low and simmer for 20 minutes if frozen beans are used. Dry beans, soaked overnight, take two hours or more of simmering to be tender, and need the additional water.
3.   Stir occasionally, adding water if necessary, until beans are done. Serve over rice with Arabic bread.

Falafel

Fava and garbanzo bean patties

◆

Although I don't remember eating this as a child, it is a food that I love and frequently make. This new recipe, inspired by a recent trip to Lebanon, incorporates Mother's recipe, suggestions from several friends, and comes with a warning: it can be addictive! Serve folded in a pocket bread with *lots* of the following: *taratour* or tahini sauce, tomatoes, and fresh mint, parsley, onions with sumac, and with pickles and *liffit* on the side. A food processor makes this very easy to make; also possible, but more difficult in a blender. An alternative to frying *falafel* is to broil them as flat patties, with sesame seeds coating them. See notes at the end of the recipe beforehand.

1 cup small dry fava beans, soaked 12-24 hours
1 cup dry garbanzo beans, soaked 12-24 hours
1/2 onion, minced
5 cloves garlic, minced or mashed into a paste
1/2 teaspoon salt
1/2 teaspoon black pepper
1 tablespoon ground coriander
2 teaspoons cumin
1/2 teaspoon paprika
1/4 teaspoon cayenne pepper
1 or 2 tablespoons flour (if needed)
1/2 teaspoon baking soda
1/2 cup parsley, minced
1/2 cup fresh cilantro, minced
1/2 cup sesame seeds (in mixture or rolled on outside)
vegetable oil, for frying
fresh chopped mint, parsley, tomatos, green onions or
  onions with sumac, for garnish

1.   Rinse beans and soak them in 1 quart of water for at least 12 hours, the longer, the better. Canned beans may be substituted for dry beans. Drain beans and rinse. Grind drained beans in

a food processor or put them through a food grinder two times.
2. Add onion, garlic and spices, baking soda, minced parsley and cilantro, mixing well. Add sesame seeds to mixture, or place them in a plate.
3. Form a spoonful of the mixture into a ball. If the consistency is correct, and the ball holds together, proceed. If not, mix in water or flour, so that you can form a ball or patty in the palm of your hands.
4. Roll ball in sesame seeds if you haven't added them to mixture. If you have a *falafel* tool, add the sesame seeds to the mixture and carefully drop the *falafel* into the heated oil with the *falafel* ejecting tool, *qalb*, as described in 5.
5. To deep fry, heat oil about two inches deep in a wok or skillet to 450-475°F. Fry *falafel* in hot oil until golden brown on both sides. Remove with slotted spoon and drain. It is possible to fry them in a small amount of oil, instead of deep frying. I have made it both ways. Serve in pocket sandwiches with fresh vegetables and plenty of tahini or *taratour* sauce.

NOTES ON SUCCESSFUL *FALAFEL*-MAKING
• The secret to *falafel* holding together in balls or patties is the consistency of the mixture. If it is too dry, it will fall apart, so add water; if it is too moist, add a little flour. Ideally you can roll it into a ball, or shape it into a patty in your hand, and it will hold together.
• Slipping the skins off the fava beans before grinding takes time and results in a perfectly textured mix in the food processor. When I did not remove the skins, the mixture was drier and needed to have some flour and water added to hold it together, but the taste was nuttier, and delicous, perhaps more nutritious.
•If using a blender to grind the beans, water must be added to make them purée. The mixture becomes too wet, so add flour to make it bind together.
•If using canned beans, it may be necessary to add flour, also.
•Make a batch or a double batch of *falafel*, form them into patties, and then freeze them individually by placing patties on a cookie sheet and into the freezer until hard, approximately an hour. Remove from freezer, place into a plastic freezer bag and back in freezer for use later, one or six at a time, for a quick meal.

Khudra

◆

Vegetables
Beans & Grains

Riz m'falfal

STEAMED RICE WITH BUTTER

◆

Buttery and rich, *riz m'falfal* was one of our family staples, the base upon which so many of the stews made with beans, vegetables and perhaps small bits of lamb were laid. Scooped up with a triangle of Arabic bread, and followed by crunchy fresh vegetables, the nutritional value is excellent, especially if made with brown rice. This recipe is based on quicker cooking white rice, so increase the cooking time twenty minutes if you use brown rice. The quantity is enough to serve our large family, so adjust the recipe in half or otherwise, unless you want a lot of leftovers!

1/4 cup clarified butter
5 cups water
1/4 teaspoon salt
3 cups rice, soaked 1 hour, drained
1/4 teaspoon cinnamon

1.   Heat clarified butter until hot. Carefully add water—it will sizzle and splatter—and salt; bring to rolling boil.
2.   Stir in rice, cover and cook on medium high heat about 10 minutes or until most of the surface water has evaporated and air bubbles form through the rice.
3.   Reduce heat to low and cook for 10 minutes more. Turn off heat and let sit for 10 minutes. Stir with fork to fluff up. Let stand 15 minutes. Serve on platter with the surface smoothed out and sprinkled with ground cinnamon.

Hommous b'Tahini

Garbanzo bean purée with tahini

◆

Our family loves *hommous* best when it is tangy, the way Mama and *Sitto* made it. We garnish it with sprinkled paprika, parsley sprigs, and a little olive oil. In Lebanon, pomegranate seeds, whole garbanzo beans and a drizzle of olive oil might be the garnish.

    2 cups dry garbanzo beans, soaked overnight
        or 2 cans garbanzo beans
    1/2 teaspoon baking soda
    4 heaping tablespoons tahini
    3 cloves of garlic
    1/2 cup lemon juice
    1/2 teaspoon salt
    2 tablespoons olive oil

1. DRY BEANS: Drain soaked beans, put in large pot, cover with 2 times the amount of water. Bring to boil and simmer over medium heat for 3/4 hour. Add baking soda. Cook over low heat until very tender. Set aside to cool. Drain and reserve liquid.

CANNED BEANS: Drain liquid from can and place beans in a pot with water to cover. Bring to a boil, reduce heat, add baking soda, and simmer for 20 minutes or until tender. Set aside to cool. Drain and reserve cooking water.

2. Mash garlic with salt into a smooth paste in a bowl; stir in tahini. Gradually stir in 1/4 cup warm water, which thickens the

tahini; stir in lemon juice and garlic paste.

3. Set aside a few whole garbanzo beans for garnish and put the remaining beans through a food mill or mash them through a strainer, blender or food processor. Add some of the cooking water to blend. Mix puréed beans into tahini mixture. Add 1/4 cup olive oil, taste and add more lemon, salt, or garlic as needed.

4. Spread into a thin layer on a flat plate, making a swirl in the surface with the back of a spoon. Then garnish with whole chick peas, parsley, paprika or mild cayenne, and olive oil drizzled over the top. Serve with Arabic bread.

QUICK BLENDER *HOMMOUS* METHOD:

Blend garlic, salt and lemon juice in the blender. Pour into a bowl. Blend the garbanzo beans, one cup at a time with 1/8 cup water. Stir this into the bowl. Stir in tahini, 1/4 cup warm water, and olive oil. Taste and add more lemon or salt, if necessary. Enjoy!

Baba ghannouj

EGGPLANT WITH TAHINI

◆

Along with *hommous*, *baba ghannouj* is one of the most popular Lebanese dishes and is becoming available in non-Middle Eastern venues, such as supermarket delis, because it is so delicious. The secret to its distinctive flavor comes from charring the eggplant directly over a flame. Dried mint adds an extra touch to our already divine family recipe, from our Douma friends, the Haddads. A must for *mezza*, *baba ghannouj*, sprinkled with pomegranate seeds, a loaf of bread, and olives make for a perfect light meal.

> 2 eggplants
> 1 tablespoon olive oil
> 1/4 cup lemon juice
> 3 cloves garlic
> 1/2 teaspoon salt
> 1/2 cup tahini
> 1 teaspoon dried mint (optional)
> fresh parsley or pomegranate seeds, for garnish

1. Set whole, unpeeled eggplant over flame until totally charred, about fifteen minutes per side—when one side is done, gently hold eggplant with wooden spoons on each end to turn it without piercing it. The marvelous charred flavor is most easily done directly over the flame of a gas stove burner—I set eggplant directly on the burner—or on a barbeque grill, or in a broiler.

2. Chop garlic, place in a medium-sized bowl and mash into a paste with salt. When eggplant is cool, slice it in half lengthwise and use a spoon to scoop pulp into the bowl, discarding large seeds and charred skin. Mash it into the garlic paste until the mixture is smooth. Mix in tahini, lemon juice, and olive oil. Add mint if you wish. Taste and adjust seasoning.

3. Spread into a thin layer on a flat plate, making a swirl in the surface with the back of a spoon. Garnish with parsley, pomegranate seeds or finely ground dried mint; drizzle with olive oil. Serve warm or cold with snippets of Arabic bread.

Batinjan m'Tabbal

EGGPLANT WITH GARLIC, OIL AND LEMON

◆

Essentially, this is *baba ghannouj* without tahini, so it is somewhat lighter and equally delicious.

2 eggplants
1 tablespoon olive oil
1/4 cup lemon juice
3 cloves garlic
1/2 teaspoon salt·

GARNISH
1/2 cup fresh parsley sprigs
1/8 cup pomegranate seeds

1. Follow *baba ghannouj* recipe through mashing the garlic into a paste in step 2. Add lemon juice and olive oil, mixing thoroughly. Taste and adjust seasoning.

2. Garnish with parsley or pomegranate seeds and drizzle with a little olive oil. Serve warm or cold with snippets of Arabic bread.

Ful m'Dammas

FAVA BEANS WITH GARLIC AND LEMON

◆

Fava beans grow in the snow and seem to withstand the weather well. They grow from Spain and France through Egypt, a staple of Mediterranean diets. My garlic-laden recipe is lemony tart and very hearty. There are two common varieties of fava beans, both are eaten fresh and dried: a huge bean dried is used in making *falafel*; a smaller fava, used for this dish, is made from the dried bean.

> 1 large can fava beans
> *or* 2 cups small dry fava beans, soaked overnight
> 6 cloves garlic, whole peeled
> 1/2 cup lemon juice
> 2 tablespoons olive oil
> 1/2 teaspoon salt
> dash of cayenne pepper
> fresh parsley for garnish

1.   Rinse soaked beans, place in a pot and add a quart of water, salt, and garlic cloves. Bring to a boil, then reduce heat and simmer for about 3 hours. If using canned beans, add 1 cup of water and garlicto beans and heat slowly for about an hour.

2.   Check and stir frequently, so that beans thicken but do not stick or burn, adding water if necessary. Some beans will break down into a very thick, soupy consistency and others remain whole.

3.   Just before serving, add lemon juice and olive oil; taste and adjust seasoning. Lots of lemon and garlic make this a heavenly dish. Garnish with parsley and serve with Arabic bread as part of *mezza,* or for breakfast or a hearty winter supper.

Lubiyeh Miqliyeh b'zeit

STRING BEANS WITH TOMATO AND OLIVE OIL

◆

String beans with tomatoes are simply delicious and easy-to-make and appeared regularly, to our delight, on our dinner table—with or without lamb—served over rice or as a side dish. A very classic Lebanese family vegetable offering.

> 2 medium onions, chopped
> 1/4 cup olive oil
> 1 1/2 pounds string beans, french cut, rinsed
> 1 medium can whole tomatoes, chopped
> 1/2 teaspoon salt
> 1/4 teaspoon black pepper
> dash cayenne pepper

    1.   Sauté onions with oil and salt in a deep skillet or sauce pan over medium heat until translucent.

    2.   Add string beans, black pepper and cayenne. Cover and cook for 5 minutes. Lower heat and steam for 15 minutes. Add tomatoes and simmer on a medium heat until tender, about 20 minutes.

    3.   Serve hot or warm over rice, *riz m'falfal* , with *khoobz*. In the summer, it is delicious served cold with bread.

Bamyia ou riz

OKRA WITH RICE

◆

Make *riz m'falfal* or steamed rice to serve with this okra delicacy, made in the summer when fresh okra are in season.

2 pounds okra, rinsed and stemmed
3 onions, julienne cut
2 cloves garlic, chopped
1/3 cup olive oil
2 small cans tomato sauce
1 teaspoon ground coriander seed
1/2 teaspoon salt
1/4 teaspoon black pepper
dash cayenne pepper
1/4 cup lemon juice
1 cup water

1. Rinse and carefully stem okra. Dry them and brush with olive oil. Broil until lightly browned.
2. Meanwhile, sauté onions lightly in remaining oil. Add okra, garlic, tomato sauce, water, lemon juice and seasonings. Stir very gently, cover and simmer for 30 minutes. Serve over rice, *riz m'falfal*, with Arabic bread.

Khudra makhluta

SAUTÉED VEGETABLES WITH *TARATOUR* SAUCE

◆

Tasty vegetables, sautéed to a golden brown that brings out their flavor, are served over steamed rice and drizzled with tahini garlic sauce—simply fabulous!

1/4 cup olive oil
1/2 cauliflower, cut into florets
2 carrots, sliced on the diagonal
2 Italian zucchini or Lebanese squash, sliced
    on the diagonal
onion or other vegetables, optional
tahini or *taratour* sauce (page 37)

    1.   Heat olive oil in a large skillet over medium heat. Stir in cauliflower and carrots, coating them with oil. Sauté for ten minutes, stirring frequently until they begin to brown.

    2.   Add squash and mix well, continue to sauté and brown. Cover, reduce heat, and steam for about ten more minutes. Meanwhile, make tahini sauce. Serve over rice or as a side vegetable, with tahini sauce.

Kousa ros

SQUASH FRITTERS

◆

An excellent summer side dish or appetizer—a fine use for some of that extra squash from the garden or the squash pulp cored from *kousa mihshi.*

> 2 cups grated squash *or* squash marrow
> from cored zucchini *kousa mihshi*
> 2 green onions, chopped
> 2 sprigs of mint, finely chopped
> 1/2 bunch of parsley, finely chopped
> 2 stalks celery, finely chopped
> 1/4 teaspoon salt
> 1/4 teaspoon black pepper
> 1/4 teaspoon cayenne
> 1/3 cup flour
> 2 1/2 teaspoons baking powder
> 1/2 cup olive oil, for frying

1. Grate squash into a bowl. If using squash marrow from cored squash for *kousa,* drain squash in a colander and reserve liquid for soup stock.

2. Squeeze mint and parsley to remove excess water and add with chopped green onions and celery to bowl. Mix it all together well along with seasonings, flour and baking powder.

3. Heat skillet with olive oil. When it is hot, spoon out a heaping teaspoon of mixture and flatten into round patties about one-half inch thick. Fry on both sides until golden brown.

4. Drain on paper towels or bags. Garnish with parsley and serve with *mezza,* brunch or as a side dish with *khoobz.*

ALICE'S KITCHEN

VEGETABLES BEANS & GRAINS

Batata Madooa Siyeme

LEBANESE MASHED POTATOES

◆

If you love mashed potatoes, you will love this recipe. These potatoes are fabulous, either served hot, warm or cold. We traditionally enjoyed them during Lent in the spring before Easter and through the summer months.

6-8 medium potatoes, peeled and quartered
1/3 cup olive oil
1/3 cup lemon juice
3 cloves garlic
1/2 teaspoon salt
3 tablespoons dried spearmint

1. Boil potatoes until tender. Meanwhile, in a small bowl, mash chopped garlic with salt into a paste; add oil and lemon juice and set aside.

2. When potatoes are tender, remove them from cooking water and reserve it. Place potatoes in a deep bowl and mash them while they are warm. Mix in garlic sauce and a little water from cooking the potatoes. Crush dried mint between your palms over the mixture and mix thoroughly. Taste and adjust seasoning. Served warm or cold.

Milayeh Schmandar, Spanegh, or Siliq

SAUTÉED BEET GREENS, SPINACH OR CHARD

◆

Spring or summer brings another favorite Lenten dish in our family from dear mother, Alice, that complements the mashed potato recipe on the previous page, lentil soups or more elaborate meals.

2 bunches spinach or greens, rinsed and drained
2 onions, chopped julienne
2 cloves garlic, minced
2 tablespoons olive oil
1/4 teaspoon salt
1/3 cup lemon juice

1.　Chop stems of greens to 2" lengths and tear greens in half. Sauté onions and garlic lightly until light brown in olive oil with salt. When onions are translucent, add stems of chard or beet greens and continue to sauté for about 5 to 7 minutes.

2.　Add leafy greens, stir and cover. Steam for 15 minutes on low. Add lemon juice. Taste and adjust seasonings. Serve hot, at room temperature or cold.

Lubiyeh M'toume

STRING BEANS WITH GARLIC LEMON OIL

◆

Whether the vegetable is string beans, spinach, asparagus, chard, beet greens, or potatoes, the garlic-laden lemon sauce poured over them is superb and can be served warm or at room temperature.

1 1/2 pounds string beans, julienne cut
2-3 cloves garlic
1/4 teaspoon salt
2 tablespoons olive oil
1/8 cup lemon juice

1.   Steam string beans in a covered pot with a cup of water until tender.

2.   Meanwhile in a small bowl, mash chopped garlic into a paste with salt. Mix in lemon juice and olive oil.

3.   Reserve bean water for cooking rice or for soup stock and place drained beans in a bowl and pour garlic sauce over them. Toss, taste and adjust seasonings.

Kousa or Batinjan Miqli
FRIED SQUASH OR EGGPLANT
◆

Almost anything fried is yummy. But memories of Mother and *Sitto* frying up squash and eggplant down in the basement on the special stove used for baking bread so the kitchen wouldn't get so hot in the summertime, make me long for this comfort food again. Salting and draining the vegetables ahead of time, draws out the liquid and keeps them from absorbing as much oil in frying. These finger-licking, quick-to disappear rounds were served with fish or *m'jaddrah* during Lent or on Fridays. We ate them tucked into Arabic bread with our meal, or as a cold sandwich, in the unlikely event that any were leftover, the next day.

> 2 large eggplants *or* 5 Japanese eggplants *or* zucchini
> salt
> olive oil for frying

1. Slice zucchini or eggplant into 1/4 inch-thick rounds. Sprinkle with salt on both sides. Place in a bowl or colander for an hour to drain. Remove from bowl, discard liquid and pat them dry.
2. Heat olive oil in a skillet; when it is hot, deep fry rounds until golden brown on each side, turning them with a fork. Place on paper towels to drain. Serve hot, warm or cold with *khoobz*.

Khoobz

◆

Breads

Bread is an essential part of every Lebanese meal, central to our diet and our culture. Traditionally Lebanese foods are eaten with torn pieces of bread formed into a triangle with three fingers as a scoop. Some foods are rolled into a sandwich or stuffed into the bread's pocket. Eating fresh baked bread, hot from the oven is an almost universal pleasure—either plain, with honey, butter, jam, yogurt, cheese, olives or with *zaa'tar.*

Arabic bread takes on a variety of forms and shapes, depending upon how it is to be baked and eaten, and the recipe, style and village of the baker. *Khoobz marouq,* big flat paper thin round loaves, is baked in an oven. In the old country there was a *tannour,* like the Indian tandoor, in which the bread, *khoobz marouq,* was baked against the vertical walls of the oven. When the bread was done, it would fall toward the fire below, requiring the baker's unwavering attention. Now there are only a few remaining *tannour* ovens in Lebanon; the *furn* is the prevailing oven for baking breads; it is much like pizza ovens fired by either gas or wood.

Saj bread is baked over a *saj,* an open fire with a domed metal disk placed over it, like an upside down wok; this ancient method of baking is being revived and becoming popular at sidewalk, take-out restaurants in Beirut. And the Lebanese *tilme* and meat and spinach pies are baked in *furn* ovens.

Commercial bakeries in the cities and larger towns produce mountains of the large *khoobz marouq* loaves on a conveyor belt sys-

tem, much like the ones I've seen in Mexico for producing corn tortillas. In the Christian Syrian town of Sidnaiye, I saw people lined up waiting for bread, just as I saw Mexicans lined up for their daily tortillas coming off the conveyor belt. But homemade breads are where my passions lie.

In this section, I provide our family recipes for baking bread, the method Mother devised for our Wedgewood gas stove. Recipes are also included for *tilme* and savory pastries. Any of these doughs may be frozen before rising for later use. Typically, I bake bread once or twice a month and freeze the baked loaves for quick thawing over an open gas flame.

When I bake, as Mother did, I make one recipe of basic bread dough, and divide the balls into various sizes for bread, *tilme b'zaa'tar*, *tilme b'kishk*, and plain *tilme*. First I bake the bread in the hot oven without the baking racks and then turn the oven down, put the racks back in, mix a small batch of *zaa'tar* and/or *kishk* and bake them; when I run out of toppings, I bake the remaining dough into pocket bread or *khoobz marouq*.

Baking bread truly nourishes the soul as much as eating it nourishes the body. I hope you enjoy and bake your own bread with these recipes. *Makoul il hanna!*

Khoobz Marouq
Basic Bread Dough
◆

Mother and *Sitto's* basic time-honored bread recipe is one we use for baking Arabic bread, either big flat loaves, or smaller, thicker pocket bread, *kmege*, for *tilme b'zaa'tar, tilme b'kishk*, or for spinach or meat pie dough. I even use it to make pizza.

3 cups warm water
1 teaspoon salt
1 tablespoon sugar
3 tablespoons dry yeast
3/4 cup wheat germ (if using only white flour)
8 cups flour (I use 3 cups whole wheat and 5 cups
    unbleached white)

1. Dissolve yeast in lukewarm water in a large bowl. Add sugar and let proof for 5 minutes. With your hand, mix in salt and three cups of the flour, removing lumps. Continue adding flour a cup at a time, kneading as you go and scraping flour from the sides of the bowl with your hand. Add more water as needed.

2. When the dough is thoroughly mixed and has a smooth, moist consistency that does not stick to your hands, divide it into 5-6 parts and shape into orange-sized balls. To make small loaves, roll into egg-sized balls. To freeze dough, see instructions below.

3.   Roll balls in flour and place on a cloth-covered flat surface allowing space between them to double in size. Cover with a damp cloth or plastic wrap and place in a warm spot to rise for one hour or until doubled. Preheat oven to 475°F.

4.   On a clean, dry, floured surface, roll out a ball of dough with a rolling pin—while one loaf is baking, begin rolling out the next one—as thick as you like: 1/8" for *khoobz marouq* or 1/4" for pocket bread *kmege*—using flour to keep dough from sticking. Here's where the twirling and tossing in the air comes in. I watch pizza bakers to learn their tricks, and remember vividly Mother's arms performing her bread dance from the days when she baked every couple of weeks for our huge, hungry family.

5.   Baking our bread happens quickly and requires undivided attention. Every oven is different, so be watchful, get to know your own oven and what works best. The hotter the oven, the quicker it puffs up and the pocket forms.

IN A GAS STOVE: place dough directly on the bottom of hot oven either on a baking tray, on a piece of foil, or on a baking stone until bread puffs up or forms air bubbles, about 5 minutes. Place in broiler for a minute until bread puffs up and lightly browns top.

IN AN ELECTRIC OVEN: place dough on a tray on the bottom oven rack until bread puffs up. Move to top rack briefly to lightly brown top.

6.   Place in damp towel to cool and soften, or eat hot and crispy. Heaven!

TO FREEZE DOUGH
Roll dough balls in flour; wrap tightly in plastic; freeze in ziplock bags. To thaw and rise: remove from bag, leave at room temperature 2 hours or in refrigerator overnight. Roll out and bake as above.

Tilme b'zeit

THICK ARABIC BREAD WITH OLIVE OIL

◆

T*ilme* can refer to bread, but also refers to a thick, foccacia-like bread that is eaten with cheese, olives, for dipping and all the usual ways bread is eaten in our cuisine. It is made with the same basic bread dough and differs in the thickness, the method of forming the loaf, and a lower baking temperature. I use this same recipe for making pizza, foccacia or *tilme*.

> basic Arabic bread dough (page 162)
> olive oil
> water

1.   Follow basic dough recipe, making dough balls as large or as small as you like—including small individual-sized rounds, through step 3. Preheat oven to 375°F.

2.   Place raised ball of dough on an oiled baking tray or a tray lined with baking parchment. Using your hand, dipped into water and olive oil, pat and flatten dough to 1/2" thick, spreading dough out from the center, leaving edges slightly thicker. Leave space between for them to rise in baking.

3.   Let dough rest 10 minutes and then bake on lower oven rack until slightly browned on the bottom. Move to top oven rack until top is very lightly browned. Cool and serve.

Tilme b' Zaa'tar or Manaishe

LEBANESE BREAD WITH ZAA'TAR

◆

One of the most unique flavors of our cuisine is *zaa'tar*, a savory combination of spices and dried herbs mixed in Lebanese villages. The mixture, composed of *zaa'tar*—variously defined as thyme, oregano, or savory!—with sumac, and sesame seeds, is baked on bread dough, and served hot or at room temperature for breakfast, lunch, appetizers or dinner. So delicious! In Lebanon, *tilme b'zaa'tar*, or *manaishe*, is eaten for breakfast right from the oven or filled with tomatoes, fresh mint leaves, green onions, or *labne* and eaten like a sandwich.

> basic Arabic bread dough (page 162)
> 1/3 cup *zaa'tar* mixture
> 1-2 tablespoons sesame seeds
> 1/3 cup olive oil

1. Follow basic dough recipe through step 3, making dough balls as large or as small as you like, even small individual-sized rounds for appetizers, *mezza*. Preheat oven to 375°F.

2. Place *zaa'tar* in a small bowl and stir in sesame seeds. Stir in olive oil and set aside, while dough is rising.

3. Place a raised ball of dough on an oiled baking tray or a tray lined with baking parchment. Flatten dough with your hand to 1" thick, spreading it out from the center, leaving edges thicker.

4. Spoon two tablespoons *zaa'tar* mix onto center; press into dough and spreading mix to 1/2" from the edge—the dough now about 1/4" thick. Fill baking tray, leaving space between each *tilme* to rise in baking. If there is extra dough, make *tilme b'zeit*.

5. Let dough rest ten minutes. Bake on bottom oven rack for 10 to 15 minutes, until bottom is slightly browned. Move to top rack until lightly browned on top. Remove from oven, cool and serve. Cut into small triangles for *mezza* or larger pieces, or serve whole, as you like.

Tilme B' Kishk

LEBANESE BREAD WITH *KISHK*

◆

Kishk is a traditional Lebanese food made by villagers in the summer for winter use. Made of *burghul*, bulgar, combined with yogurt, *laban*, it is laboriously ground by hand into coarse flour. Here, it is applied to *tilme*, and makes a pizza-like savory bread that is excellent. *Kishk* can be purchased from Middle East groceries.

> basic Arabic bread dough (page 162)
> 2 cups *kishk*
> 1 cup olive oil
> 1 onion, finely chopped
> 1 tomato, finely chopped

1.   Follow basic dough recipe, making dough balls as large or as small as you like—including small individual-sized rounds, through step 3.

2.   Preheat oven to 375°F. Place *kishk* in a small bowl and stir in olive oil, onion and tomato. Mix well and set aside.

3.   Place a raised ball of dough on an oiled baking tray or a tray lined with baking parchment. First flatten dough with your hand to 1 inch thick, spreading it out from the center, leaving edges slightly thicker.

4.   Spoon a couple of tablespoons *kishk* mixture and press into dough, spreading to 1/2" from the edge, with dough now about 1/4 inch thick. Continue filling tray, leaving space between each *tilme* to rise in baking.

5.   Let dough rest ten minutes. Bake on bottom oven rack for 10 to 15 minutes or until bottom is slightly browned. Move to top rack until lightly browned on top. Remove from oven, cool or serve hot from oven. Cut into small triangles for *mezza* or larger pieces, or serve whole, as you like.

Hillou

◆

Sweets

Attar

SIMPLE FRAGRANT SYRUP

◆

Attar, our light, fragrant syrup is used in many of our dessert recipes. Make some ahead of time to have on hand in the refrigerator, as our recipes require it chilled. This recipe makes approximately a cup of syrup.

> 1 1/2 cups sugar
> 1 1/2 cups water
> 1/3 cup lemon juice
> 1 teaspoon *may warid* or *may zahar*

1.   Put water, sugar and lemon juice in a saucepan and cook over medium heat, stirring frequently, until mixture thickens into a syrupy consistency. This may take 45 minutes.

2.   Cool and add *may zahar* or *may warid*. Decant into a glass bottle and chill.

Atayif b'jouz

LEBANESE CREPES WITH CHEESE OR WALNUT FILLING

◆

Similar to French crepes, these excellent Lebanese filled pastries can be enjoyed as evening desserts or, as they are typically served in Lebanon, for breakfast or brunch. The delicate orange flower water, *may zahar*, flavor makes them irresistible. Note that *atayif* may be fried or baked and can be made ahead and stored in the freezer to bake or fry at the last minute. Make *attar* syrup ahead and chill, recipe previous page.

1 cup *attar* syrup, cold

CHEESE FILLING
 1 pint ricotta cheese
  or 2 cups arishe (page 31)
 1 1/2 cups grated jack cheese
 1 1/2 tablespoons sugar
 1 tablespoon *may zahar*

WALNUT FILLING
 2 cups chopped walnuts
 2 tablespoons sugar
 2 tablespoons *may zahar*

DOUGH/BATTER
 2 cups flour
 2 1/2 cups water
 1/2 tablespoon yeast
 1 teaspoon sugar
 1/8 teaspoon baking soda
 1/2 teaspoon salt
 vegetable oil and clarified butter, for frying

1.   Dissolve yeast in lukewarm water with sugar and let proof 5 minutes in a deep mixing bowl. Combine salt and baking

soda with flour and gradually stir into water, removing any lumps that form. The correct consistency is like a thin pancake batter. Cover and place in a warm place to rise for 1/2 to one hour or until doubled in size.

2. Meanwhile, make either or both fillings by mixing ingredients in separate bowls.

3. Heat a griddle coated lightly with olive oil on medium temperature. If batter is too thick, thin it with a little water. Pour batter into 3" to 4" rounds, about 1/8" thick. Cook only on one side until the surface has air bubbles and is not wet or shiny and the bottom is golden brown, like a pancake. Set them on a plate and cover with a tea towel. Fill those that are done as described in step 4, while others are cooking on the griddle.

4. Fill each dough circle with about a teaspoon of either cheese or nut filling on the uncooked side and pinch edges together, forming a fat half circle. Set aside to fry or bake.

To DEEP FRY

Heat oil and clarified butter in a frying pan. When it is hot, drop in *atayif* and brown on each side for about 3 to 4 minutes. This may take slightly longer if they have been frozen. Lift out and drain on paper for a minute. Place on a platter and drizzle cold attar syrup over while they are still quite hot. Serve immediately.

To BAKE

Preheat oven to 350°F. Place *atayif* in a pyrex baking tray dotted with a little clarified butter. Bake for approximately 30 minutes. If they have been frozen, bake for 45 minutes. Remove from oven and immediately drizzle cold *attar* syrup over them and serve.

Mamool

Walnut filled cookies

These traditional Easter cookies are made in Lebanon in press molds. Mother and *Sitto* preferred to devise their own method of decorating these scrumptious nut-filled cookies. Mother commissioned a sheet metal worker to cut out and form several pincers, *malqat,* which we use to decorate *mamools* and date-filled and other cookies. *Mamools* are not difficult to make, but like all good things, take time, so invite some friends over or bring your children 'round you and have fun filling, pinching and decorating together! The first step is done 5 hours ahead. Once they are baked, eating them will be as pleasing as making them.

Filling—Mix together
    3 cups finely chopped walnuts
    2 tablespoons *may zahar*
    1/3-1/2 cup sugar

Dough
    2 cups farina, *smeed*, or cream of wheat
    1 1/4 cups melted clarified butter, *samne m'fatse*
    1/2 teaspoon *mahlab*, ground
    1/2 cup milk
    1/2 tablespoon dry yeast
    1 1/2 cups flour

1/2 cup sugar

2 tablespoons *may zahar*

T*OPPING*

1/2 cup powdered sugar

1.   In a mixing bowl, pour warm melted butter over farina and *mahlab*. Let stand approximately 5 hours.

2.   Dissolve yeast in 1/4 cup of warm milk. Heat remaining milk almost to boil, pour over farina mixture and let cool for 10 minutes.

3.   Mix flour into farina mixture. Knead in yeast and milk mixture. Add *may zahar* and knead well to achieve a uniform, elastic, moist dough, adding more flour if needed. Cover and put in a warm place to rest for 1/2 hour before forming cookies.

4.   Preheat oven to 350°F.

5.   Form a ball of dough 1 1/2" in diameter in the palm of your hands. Use the palm of your left hand to support the ball while making a cup or hollow by pressing the dough to an even thickness using your right index finger.

6.   Place roughly 1 teaspoonful of filling into hollow and pinch closed, reshaping it into a round form between your palms. Use *malat* (pincers) to make a design on cookie, place on cookie sheet and bake for 1/2 hour until ever so slightly brown. Bake for 10 minutes on bottom rack, and the remaining time on top rack.

7.   Cool cookies completely and then sift powdered sugar over the tops and serve or store in airtight tins.

Caak b'simsom

SESAME COOKIES

◆

Sesame covered, crisp and light, with the subtle richness of *mahlab* flavor, we couldn't get enough of these cookies! *Sitto* and Mother let me help make them—rolling dough, lifting the fragile dough circles out of a pool of milk, and dropping them onto the beach of sesame seeds. Our sesame cookies are a perfect accompaniment to tea or coffee, and are a great baking project to do with children, who love to cook, given the opportunity.

TOPPING

    1/2 cup milk

    1/4 cup sugar

    1-2 cups sesame seeds

1. Mix milk and sugar together in a bowl and set aside.
2. Put sesame seeds in a wide shallow bowl and set aside.

DOUGH

    3 cups flour

    2 teaspoons baking powder

    3/4 cup sugar

    1 teaspoon *mahlab*, ground

    3/4 cup clarified butter *or* 1/2 pound butter, melted

    1 egg

    3/4 cup milk

1. Mix dry ingredients together in a bowl. Pour in butter and mix thoroughly.
2. Beat egg with milk and knead into dough. Consistency desired is moist, not sticky. Add flour if needed to achieve this.
3. Preheat oven to 350°F.
4. Take a small piece of dough and roll it between your palms to form a pen-like shape, 1/3 inch by 7 inches long. Pinch

ends of the dough together, with a half inch overlap, making a circle about two to three inches across, with a hole in the center.

5.   Drop circle into milk and sugar mixture for a moment, coating the dough. Carefully lift it out with a fork and drop it into the sesame seeds; flip it over, covering entire cookie with seeds which adhere to the surface. Using the fork, place cookie onto a baking tray lined with parchment, and shape it into a circle again, leaving a little space between each cookie to rise.The dough is soft, pliable, and is easily shape at this stage.

6.   Bake for 10 to 15 minutes until lightly browned and crisp. Cool completely before storing.These will store for a few weeks in an airtight container, if they are out of sight!

Caak b' Haleeb

ANISE COOKIES WITH MILK

◆

The flavors of anise and *mahlab* impart subtle fragrance to another Lebanese classic pastry. Dense, thick cookies, that are more like cake or bread, *caak b'haleeb* have a wonderful olive oil flavor and a chewy texture. They are simple both in making and in their elegance; they are not frequently seen outside Lebanese circles, so they would be an interesting and easy dessert to make for guests.

1 tablespoon yeast
1/4 cup warm water
1/2 cup sugar
1 cup olive oil
2 tablespoons anise seeds, finely ground
1/2 teaspoon *mahlab*, freshly ground
1/2 teaspoon salt
3 cups flour
1/4 cup milk

1. Dissolve yeast in lukewarm water and set aside to proof.
2. Meanwhile, in a mixing bowl cream together oil with sugar. Add *mahlab*, anise, salt and flour, mixing thoroughly with your hands. Knead in yeast and water mixture. Slowly mix in enough milk so that the consistency becomes smooth but not sticky. Cover and let rest a half hour.
3. Divide dough into 3 balls and let rest another half hour. Preheat oven to 350°F.
4. Form into little balls, about the size of a golf ball, and flatten to 2"-3" wide circles that are 1/4" thick. Pinch edges like a pie crust and press a fork across the top, to create a design on the surface and keep the cookie flat. Place on baking tray and bake for 15 minutes, about 7 minutes on the bottom rack and finishing on the top, until lightly golden in color. Cool thoroughly and store.

ALICE'S KITCHEN
SWEETS

Graibee

SHORTBREAD COOKIES

◆

Crisp and light, these classic Lebanese shortbread cookies melt in your mouth! Our tradition is to have cookies only during the Christmas holidays served with tea or Arabic coffee. Every year in the weeks before Christmas, Mother still bakes up a storm and puts together beautiful gift boxes that include these and a variety of her other sweets, stuffed dates and homemade candies.

    1 cup clarified butter, softened
    1 cup superfine sugar
    1 1/2 cups flour
    1 egg white
    1 cup blanched almonds, split in half
        or whole pistachio *or* pine nuts, for top

1. Cream the butter until fluffy. Gradually add sugar and then egg white, continuing to blend. Add flour and mix well, adding more flour as needed so dough doesn't stick to your hands.
2. Preheat oven to 325°F.
3. Shape into balls the size of a walnut and place on ungreased baking sheet. Make an indentation in the center of each by pressing a blanched almond half into the top, flattening the cookie a little. Or roll into a coil and join ends forming a small donut shape with a hole in the center.
4. Bake lightly for 15 to 20 minutes in center oven rack until bottoms are ever so slightly golden; the tops remain white. Cool for ten minutes before moving from baking tray and then thoroughly before storing or serving. Store in airtight tins to keep crisp.

Nus Qamar

ALMOND CRESCENT MOONS

◆

Mother's secret recipe, these delicious almond crescent moons are so light and crispy, they are irresistible!

3/4 pound butter
3/4 cup sugar
1 teaspoon vanilla extract
1 teaspoon almond extract
3 cups sifted flour
2 cups ground almonds

1. Cream butter and sugar. Add vanilla, almond, and gradually stir in flour. Add more flour if dough sticks to your hands.

2. Preheat oven to 325°F.

3. Roll a tablespoon of dough between your palms to elongate it. Pinch the eges to slight points and place on baking tray curving it into a crescent moon shape, each one about 2 inches long by 1/2 inch across at the thick center. Fill tray with moons, leaving 1/2 inch between each to rise.

4. Bake on center oven rack for 15 to 20 minutes until lightly golden. Cool completely before storing.

Harist il'Louz or Nammoura

GROUND ALMOND AND FARINA PASTRY

◆

Moist, dense and cake-like, this almond-rich pastry, *nammoura* is easy enough for a child to make and tastes terrific. Even though it will keep, this pastry is at its best when freshly made. Make *attar* syrup ahead and chill, page 168.

> 4 1/2 cups farina
> 1 cup finely ground almonds, ground in blender
> 1 3/4 cups sugar
> 3 teaspoons baking powder
> 1 tablespoon *may zahar,* orange flower water
> 2 cups milk
> 1 cup clarified butter, warm (page 35)
> 3 tablespoons sesame tahini oil or sesame oil,
> to grease 13" x 18" baking tray
> 1/2 cup almonds, blanched and split in half,
> to decorate top
> 1 cup *attar* syrup, for top after baking

1. Preheat oven to 375°F. Mix dry ingredients well.
2. Add *may zahar* to milk and pour into dry ingredients. Mix well and stir in butter, mixing thoroughly. Spread mixture into greased baking tray, smoothing out top with a spatula, about 1/2 inch thick. If a smaller baking tray is used, the cookies will be thicker. Cut into small diamonds, the same as for *kibbe*, page 79. Place a blanched almond half into each diamond.
3. Place tray on lower oven rack and bake for about 15 minutes, until edges just begin to brown.
4. Move to top oven rack for 10 minutes so top will turn a light golden brown. Remove from oven and quickly recut. Immediately drizzle cold *attar* evenly over the top of pastry while still hot. Let cool for an hour and then serve.

Asabi' b'Ajwe

DATE FINGERS

◆

In these delectable cookies, dates, figs or any other fruit preserve fill a buttery, short dough. Following is the recipe for date filling, but two or so cups apricot, quince, or fig jam would nicely substitute for dates. Sometimes Mother Alice uses a mixture of jams, whatever she has on hand—Mmmmm!

DATE FILLING
> 3 cups chopped dates
> 2 cups water
> 2 tablespoons clarified butter, unmelted

DOUGH
> 1 pound softened butter (not clarified)
> > or 1/2 pound butter and 1/2 pound margarine
> 2 eggs
> 1 jigger (2-3 tablespoons) brandy
> 1/2 teaspoon ground *mahlab*
> 5 cups flour
> 3/4 cup sugar

DATE FILLING
    1.   Cook dates in saucepan with water for 20 minutes over medium heat, stirring occasionally.

    2.   Stir in butter and add a little more water if necessary, cooking until it becomes a thick paste. Set aside to cool, while making dough.

DOUGH
    1.   Cream together butter and sugar in a mixing bowl. Beat in eggs and stir in brandy and *mahlab*. Slowly stir in flour, mixing well until dough does not stick to your hands, but is not dry or stiff, adding flour as needed.

    2.   Preheat oven to 325°F.

3.   Roll a piece of dough into a 1 1/4 inch ball in the palm of your hands. Holding dough cupped in the palm of your left hand, press your index finger of the right hand into the ball, making a hollow in the dough, forming an even thickness of dough 1/8 inch. This is similar to mamool, pictured on page 171, except it is an elongated shape, rather than round.

4.   With a small spoon or fork, place approximately one teaspoon of filling into the dough and pinch it closed. Gently roll the filled dough between your palms, into an elongated shape, with pointed ends and a thick middle.

4.   Use *malat*, pincers, to decorate, place on cookie sheet and bake for 15 minutes on bottom oven rack until slightly golden on the bottom, then on top rack to brown for another 10 minutes or so. Cool thoroughly before storing or serving.

Awamee

FRIED LEBANESE DOUGHNUTS

◆

A*wamee* were an unusually sweet and decadent winter holiday treat for our family. The potato flour used in Mother's recipe makes the dough light. *Awamee* means floating, since when they are fried, they float to the top of the pot. They are lighter than doughnuts or fritters, and are dipped quickly into cold *attar* syrup, which is made ahead and chilled. Serve with Arabic coffee or tea.

1 cup *attar* syrup, chilled (page 168)

3 cups water, lukewarm
1 tablespoon yeast
1 teaspoon sugar
3 cups flour (2 cups unbleached white and
    1 cup potato flour)
1/4 teaspoon baking soda
1/2 teaspoon salt
3 cups equal parts olive oil and vegetable oil, for frying

1. Dissolve yeast in lukewarm water with sugar in a mixing bowl and let proof for 5 minutes.
2. Combine salt and baking soda with flour. Gradually stir this into the yeast mixture, until a pancake batter consistency is achieved. Cover and let rise for a half hour or until doubled in size.
3. Heat oil in a deep skillet to quite hot. Drop spoonfuls of dough into oil to fry until lightly browned. An oiled spoon allows the batter to slide right off.
4. Lift *awamee* out with a slotted spoon and immediately dip for a minute into cold *attar* syrup.

ALICE'S KITCHEN
SWEETS

Zlebiyeh

LEBANESE FRITTERS

◆

Mother's Lebanese fritters are eggless and light. Powdered sugar dusting the top imparts a delicate sweetness to a remarkably basic, nonetheless satisfying treat. Taste them both ways—without powdered sugar and with, to see which you prefer.

4 cups flour, unbleached
1/2 teaspoon salt
3 teaspoons baking powder
3 tablespoons olive oil
1 cup warm water
1/2 cup vegetable oil, for frying
powdered sugar, for top

1. Mix dry ingredients together. Add olive oil to water and mix with dry ingredients to make dough, adding a little more water or flour, as needed.
2. Form four balls of dough the size of an orange. Roll in flour, cover and let rest in a warm place for a half hour.
3. On a clean dry surface, roll dough to 1/4 inch thick and cut into 1 x 3 inch strips.
4. Heat oil in a frying pan. As *zlebiyeh* strips deep fry in hot vegetable oil, they puff up and turn light golden brown. Gently turn to brown other side.
5. Place on paper towel to drain, sprinkle with powdered sugar on all sides while warm and serve. Only cook as many as you will serve at a time. The remaining dough can be refrigerated for several days or frozen for later use.

Baklawa

BAKLAWA

◆

Unlike the weighty, honey-laden, sticky, too sweet baklava one finds commercially outside of the Middle East, our *baklawa* is so scrumptious and unheavy that it is difficult to eat just one. And it's rather easy to create, so if you've never baked this heavenly dessert, give it a go! Our family had this pastry during the Christmas season. Tins filled with baklawa are treasured gifts. Make *attar* syrup ahead and chill. If you have access to an old-fashioned nut grinder, this is the best way of grinding nuts to the desired coarseness, and avoiding the overgrinding and resulting release of oils that can happen so quickly in a blender or food processor.

> 1 cup cold *attar* syrup (page 168)
> 1 package filo dough

FILLING

> 3 cups walnuts or pistachio nuts
> 1 pound clarified butter, melted
> 1/2 cup sugar
> 2 tablespoons *may zahar*, orange flower water

1.   Coarsely grind nuts in a nut chopper and place in a bowl. Mix in sugar and *may zahar*.

2. Preheat oven to 225°F.

3. Butter 8 x 13 inch baking tray, using a pastry brush. Divide filo dough into two equal parts and begin layering individual sheets of filo dough into the baking tray and brushing each layer with butter. Continue until half of the filo dough remains.

4. Spread the nut filling evenly to the edge, covering the filo. Cover the nuts with a sheet of filo and continue layering the remaining filo, brushing each sheet with butter as above. With a sharp knife, cut pastry into lengthwise strips about one and a half inches wide, being sure to cut through all layers to the bottom of the tray. Then make another series of parallel cuts at 45 degrees, also one and a half inches wide creating diamond shapes.

5. Bake for two hours or until golden brown on top and bottom. Remove from heat and immediately drizzle cold syrup evenly over the top. Cool and reslice to serve.

Booza

LEBANESE ICE CREAM

◆

If you have ever tasted Lebanese ice cream, you've experienced its incomparable flavor and texture. During hot Los Angeles summers, Mother and Dad pulled out the ice cream maker, the rock salt, and the precious *sahlab* and *miski* in little packets from Lebanon and began the magical process. The distinctive flavor of *sahlab* is slightly more subtle but no less unusual than that of *miski*, the pine resin from Lebanon's magnificent *snobar*, pine trees. *Miski*, in addition to imparting a resonant flavor, also creates the resinous, gummy texture unique to Lebanese ice cream. There is nothing like it this side of Beirut.

At first we used an old hand-crank, labor-intensive ice cream maker and a huge block of ice that we chipped with an ice pick, but eventually we moved on to an electric spinning model and bags of ice cubes. Whichever method you use, *sahteyn!* Before you begin, check the size of the ice cream maker; if it holds a gallon of ice cream, you can triple this recipe and fill the ice cream maker to three-quarters full. If you only want a half-gallon of ice cream, just double the recipe. This recipe makes a quart.

1 quart whole milk
1 tablespoon *sahlab*
1 cup sugar
1/2 teaspoon *miski,* ground with 2 tablespoons sugar

ice cream machine
2 cups rock salt
3 bags of ice cubes or 2 blocks of ice

1. Heat milk slowly in a deep pot. Mix sugar and *sahlab* and add slowly to warm milk, stirring constantly until it thickens.
2. Meanwhile, grind *miski* with sugar in a mortar and

pestle until fine. Put through a strainer to remove coarse pieces and add gradually to thickened custard, mixing well and removing lumps. Cook five more minutes and remove from heat. Cool.

3. Put custard in ice cream maker to 3/4 full. Pack freezer alternately with rock salt and ice per instructions with ice cream maker. Allow the pack to stand for 3 minutes before you start turning. Churn for fifteen minutes, adding more ice and salt so it remains filled to the top. Be sure to stay with electric ice cream makers, because as soon the ice cream hardens enough to stop turning, it must be unplugged or the motor will burn up.

4. Pour off the salt water and wipe off lid. Remove the dasher carefully, keeping salt or water from getting into the ice cream. Place a cork in the lid and replace the lid. Repack the container in the freezer adding more salt and ice; cover with newspapers. Let stand for an hour or two. Transfer to pint or quart containers and put in freezer to harden. Enjoy!

Ammah

WHEAT BERRY PORRIDGE

◆

Cold winter nights by the fire accompanied by a bowl of *ammah* warms the spirits and the soul. *Ammah* means wheat in Arabic, but traditional American hot cereals do not compare with this brothy blend, which can be a nutritious winter evening dessert, with the leftovers easily heated for a quick, hearty breakfast. Nuts and raisins provide complementary proteins and iron, while the anise seeds impart flavor and help digestion. Our family had it winter evenings and it was served at our church in paper cups with nuts and already sweetened for memorial Masses. The consistency can vary from as dry as steamed rice to a soupy broth—terrific any way in between.

1 1/2 cups whole wheat berries, *ammah*, rinsed
4 cups water
1 tablespoon anise seeds
1/2 cup walnut pieces
1/2 cup raisins
sugar or honey

1.   Put wheat berries in a medium sized pot with water and anise seeds. Cover and bring to a boil. Reduce heat and simmer for 1 1/2 to 2 hours, stirring occasionally, and adding water if necessary.

2.   When wheat berries are fully cooked and tender, serve in bowls with cooking broth. Sugar, honey, walnut pieces, and raisins are offered in bowls to each person so they may sweeten their *ammah* to taste, and add walnut pieces and raisins, as they choose.

Knafee b'jibn

FILO CHEESECAKE WITH ORANGE FLOWER & ROSE WATER SYRUP

◆

1 pound shredded filo dough, *kataify* or *qataayif*
3/4 cup clarified butter, melted
1 cup cold syrup, *attar* (page 168)

FILLING

2 pints ricotta cheese
    or 4 cups *arishe* (page 31)
1 1/2 pounds jack cheese, grated
3 tablespoons sugar
1 teaspoon each *may zahar* and *may warid*

1. Cut dough into 1" lengths with scissors or a knife into a bowl. Drizzle warm clarified butter over dough, thoroughly blending butter into the dough between your palms—Mother says for at least 5 minutes.
2. Spread half of the dough over the bottom of an 8 x 13 inch pyrex baking tray.
3. Preheat oven to 350°F.
4. Combine filling ingredients together in a bowl and mix well. Gently spread filling to cover the bottom layer of dough. Add remaining dough to cover filling. Bake for 35 to 45 minutes, until top is light brown.
5. Remove from heat and immediately drizzle cold syrup evenly over the top. Serve at once.

Riz ib Haleeb

RICE PUDDING

◆

Comfort food if there ever was one, *riz ib haleeb*, a classic Mediterranean pudding with Lebanon's particular flavorings: orange flower water, rose water, and cinnamon. Cool and refreshing, our recipe is not too sweet. Steam rice ahead of time.

> 2 cups steamed white short grain rice, without salt
> 1 quart milk
> 2 tablespoons cornstarch
> 1/2 cup sugar
> pinch salt
> 1/2 teaspoon each *may zahar* and *may warid*
> 2 teaspoons ground cinnamon, for topping

1.   Mix together all ingredients except *may zahar*, *may warid*, and cinnamon in a sauce pan. Separate grains of rice with a spoon.

2.   Cook on stove top stirring frequently over medium heat, until milk thickens, for about a half hour. Remove from heat and add *may zahar* and *may warid*.

3.   Pour into individual pudding dishes and cool. Refrigerate to set pudding.

4.   Serve chilled with a dusting of powdered cinnamon on the top.

M'hallabiyeh

ROSE WATER PUDDING

◆

Perfumed with orange flower and rose waters, this smooth, cool, delicate pudding is sprinkled with cookie crumbs and crunchy ground nuts. It is an unusual, refreshing and memorable Middle Eastern dessert.

1 quart milk
1/2 cup corn starch
1 cup sugar
1/2 teaspoon each *may zahar* and *may warid*
2 cups cookie crumbs, for topping
2 cups ground pistachio nuts or walnuts, for topping

1. Add 2 tablespoons of milk to corn starch in a small bowl and blend.
2. Put liquefied cornstarch into a sauce pan with all of the milk and sugar. Heat over low heat, stirring until the mixture thickens, for about twenty minutes. If it doesn't thicken, dissolve one packet of plain gelatin powder into the mixture.
3. Remove from heat and stir in *may zahar* and *may warid*. Pour into a pyrex tray or into individual pudding dishes. Sprinkle cookie crumbs and ground pistachio nuts or walnuts on the top. Refrigerate to set pudding. Serve chilled.

Murabba

◆

Preserves

Mama and *Sitto* frequently made superb jams and preserves—a regular feature on our table along with bread, cheese and olives. The making of jams, fruit preserves, and molasses are traditional methods to preserve fruit, as is drying. In Douma, many houses had flat roof tops, which were warm and dry through the summer months; here, garden vegetables, grains, herbs, fruits, seeds and nuts were dried for winter use on woven drying trays or strung to hang and dry indoors.

Herbs were dried for cooking, such as spearmint, thyme, *zaa'tar*, and sumac, and for teas. Since Lebanon was on the Spice Road between the Far East and Europe, many East Asian spices came into Lebanese culinary use, such as cinnamon and peppers, that were not native to western Asia. Vegetables like okra, eggplant, pumpkin seeds, and tomatoes were dried. Tomatoes were also made into a paste, dried and stored in earthenware crocks. Vegetables and fruits were pickled to preserve them, from turnips and eggplants to watermelon rind.

Grains and legumes like corn, fava and garbanzo beans, and lentils, too, were made to last through the winter. Some were cooked whole like *ammah* or wheat, which was also taken to the mill, *baidar*, and ground into bulgar or flour. The grain mill was near the olive mill, *maasra*, next to uncle Ishaac El Hage's home, where olives were pressed into oil, a fabulous preservation alternative to salt curing, and so useful in that delectable form. The pits from the

pressed olives are packed into blocks and are still used as winter home heating fuel. Ancient stone terraces hold soil and olive trees that course down the mountainsides and provide the oil and fruits so cherished by our people. In a town near Douma are olive trees with trunks that span six feet in diameter, said to be 2000 years old.

Fruits and nuts, brought in from the coast, the desert or the south, such as *bahlah*, fresh dates—quite divine, and *tamr*, dried dates, *fistook*, pistachio nuts, apricots, *mish moosh,* bananas, oranges and citrus rounded out what was not grown in the mountains. Figs, *teen*, apples, persimmons, pomegranates and pears are abundant in Douma, as are grapes which are made into raisins or *dibbis*, grape molasses, or are fermented to make anise liquor, *arak*.

Being in Lebanon in the early fall allowed me fabulous first-taste experiences along with fresh dates and *dibbis*: fresh pistachio nuts brought in from the east whose gorgeous magenta sleeve enveloping the fresh nuts are the inspiration for the red dye sometimes seen on pistachio nut shells sold in the U.S.—Aha!

Returning from my excursion to the old country and back to our family cookbook: included in this section are our most loved jams, that, spread onto a little Arabic bread, made for a fine dessert. The secret of these jams is in using tree ripened fruit. Enjoy!

Teen ma'oud

Fig jam with anise and walnuts

◆

Along with the aromatic flavor of anise seeds, the most important secret of our recipe is to use tree-ripened figs. They can be dried first and they can be figs of any color. The jam is delicious on Arabic bread or sesame crackers for breakfast or dessert. It is also an excellent alternative for filling date cookies, *asabi' b'ajwe*.

> 10-20 ripe figs (2-3 cups)
> 1/4 -1/2 cup sugar
>   use less if figs are really oozy sweet, *dablooni*
> 1 tablespoon anise seeds
> 2 tablespoons lemon juice
> 1/2 cup chopped walnuts (optional)
> 1/4 teaspoon *miski* ground into a powder
>   with 1/2 teaspoon sugar (optional)
> 2 tablespoons sesame seeds (optional)

1. Cut off stems and chop figs into quarters, and place into two quart sauce pan. Sprinkle sugar and anise seed on top of figs without stirring. Cover and let stand overnight, forming a syrup in the bottom.

2. Add lemon juice and stir. Begin to cook slowly over low heat for several hours, until figs make a thick paste, stirring from time to time.

3. Remove from heat and set aside to cool overnight.

4. Cook again on low heat for a half hour to an hour more, stirring frequently to avoid burning or sticking. Add walnuts, sesame seeds and *miski,* if you desire, and cook for ten more minutes.

5. Can in sterile jars or cool and place in clean jars and refrigerate. Refrigerated jam can be stored several months, if enough moisture has been removed from figs during the cooking process.

Sfargel ma'oud

QUINCE JAM

◆

Quince are very high in natural pectin and our preserves are appealing, thick and beautifully colored red brown.

    6 quince, rinsed
    3 cups sugar
    3 cups water
    3 tablespoons lemon juice
    1/4 teaspoon *miski*, ground with 1 tablespoon sugar

1. Peel quince and chop into shoestrings about 1/8" thick, reserving peelings and core of quince. Place quince in deep pot with sugar on top. Let stand overnight at room temperature. In the meantime, cook peelings and cores with water for an hour. Strain liquid and reserve, discarding the pulp.

2. Begin cooking quince the next day on medium flame until tender, for an hour or so.

3. Stir in juice from peelings and continue cooking until quince is done. The color is translucent and deep, reddish brown; the liquid has turned to a thick sauce. Add lemon juice and *miski* and cook for 5 minutes. Place in sterilized jars and seal or refrigerate in clean jars for short term use.

Mishmosh

Apricot Jam

◆

Our apricot jam is distinctive because it is not overly sweet and has the fresh tartness of lemon. In addition, *Sitto's* recipe includes the almond-flavored, crunchy apricot kernels or nuts, which are found hidden in the center of the pit. This laetrile-laden, purportedly cancer-preventative nut, adds a wonderfully delicious crunchy texture to the jam, and is well worth the time it takes to hammer each apricot pit open to uncover the nut from its hard shell. I like doing this outside, like *Sitto* did, sitting on the back step, with a hammer and eye protection. The jam is incomparable on toast without any butter, and makes a great glaze for apple tarts, cakes or other confections.

> 6 cups fresh ripe, pitted apricots, rinsed and halved
> with pits reserved
> 2 cups sugar
> 1/8 cup lemon juice

1. Place apricots in deep pot with sugar on top. Let stand overnight.

2. Meanwhile, carefully crack open the apricot pits with a hammer and remove the nuts hidden within, without crushing them, if possible. Place nuts in a small pot of water and boil for about 10 minutes, which removes the bitterness. Drain the nuts and slip the skins off. Discard skins and set nuts aside.

3. Stir the jam and begin to cook it over a low flame for a couple of hours.

4. Add nuts to the jam and continue cooking down until jam thickens. This can take several hours, over several days. Be sure to stir and avoid burning the bottom as it thickens.

5. Add lemon juice toward the end of the cooking. This enhances the flavor and is a natural preservative. Can in sterile jars or refrigerate for immediate use.

Alice's Kitchen

Jlunt ou Jazar Halaweh Jazzariyeh
PUMPKIN & CARROT PRESERVE
◆

2 cups grated pumpkin
1 cup grated carrots
1 cup sugar
2 tablespoons lemon juice
1 rose geranium leaf, 'utar
    or 1 teaspoon rose geranium water

1.   Place pumpkin and carrots in a bowl with sugar on top and let stand overnight.

2.   Strain off sugar syrup that has formed and squeeze all liquid from pulp into a 1 quart sauce pan. Set pulp aside.

3.   Add lemon juice to syrup and bring to a hard boil. Stir in pulp and rose geranium leaf and continue cooking over low heat, stirring frequently, until pulp cooks and liquid thickens.

4.   If rose geranium leaf is used, remove it; if not, stir in rose geranium water for flavoring at this point. Cool and refrigerate in clean jars.

Amardine

DRIED APRICOT LEATHER

◆

The most basic way of preserving food is by naturally and simply drying it, as in this recipe for making apricot leather.

1 or 2 pounds fresh apricots, rinsed and pitted

1. Put rinsed, unpeeled, pitted apricots into a blender and blend until totally puréed. Spread purée evenly with a spatula about 1/8 to 1/4 inch thick on an oiled wooden board or a cookie sheet lined with clear plastic or baking parchment.
2. Cover with screen or cheese cloth and leave in the sun to dry if you live in a warm climate or use a commercial food dehydrator or gas oven with pilot. When the top side has dried, turn over to dry other side. Leather must be thoroughly dry to avoid spoiling. Once it is totally dry, store in waxed paper in a dry place or in a plastic bag or a tin.

Shrab

◆

Beverages

An invitation to a Lebanese home includes at the minimum an offering of a beverage—fruit juice of any kind, pineapple, orange, grape, fresh blackberry, lemonade. Arabic coffee or tea along with a sweet, *hillou*, are typically presented.

Shay

TEA

Wonderful herb teas can be made from boiling the following for ten minutes: fennel seeds and cinnamon stick; cinnamon stick; anise seeds; or steeping herbs in hot water for five minutes: mint leaves, fresh or dried; camomile flowers.

◆

Ahwe turkiyeh

ARABIC OR TURKISH COFFEE

Arabic coffee is easy to make if you have the right grind of coffee, a little *raqwi* pot, and demitasse coffee cups to serve it in. A few cardamom pods give a lovely fragrance and flavor to the coffee.

    1.   To make six cups of coffee, fill *raqwi* with 6 demitasse cups of water and 3 teaspoons of sugar. Place on medium heat and bring to a boil.

    2.   Remove from heat and stir in 6 heaping teaspoons of Arabic coffee (espresso grind) and cardamom, if desired. Return to heat and bring to a full rolling boil, lifting it from heat and stirring so it does not spill over. This may be repeated two more times.

3. Spoon a little of the froth from the top into each demitasse cup and then fill each cup with Arabic coffee. Serve with Lebanese pastries or alone, but be sure to read coffee grounds in each cup to entertain your guests, when the cups are empty.

◆

Limonada

LEMONADE

We drank gallons of lemonade in the warm southern California summers, each glass made with 1/2 cup lemon juice and the rest water, sweetened with sugar, chilled with ice, and most importantly scented with a fresh sprig of spearmint. My sister and I set up a stand out in front of the house and sold our lemonade to passers-by. They loved its flavor, just as we loved collecting those nickels!

◆

Assir l'burdon

ORANGE JUICE

Fresh squeezed orange juice is the Lebanese way to start the day, healthy, pure and simple, when they are in season.

◆

Assir l'rimman

POMEGRANATE JUICE

I drank fresh squeezed pomegranate juice in Damascus, made by a street vendor with a mountain of pomegranates on his cart. He used an old orange juicer with a lever, and put half a pomegranate where the orange normally goes, and smoosh! a fabulous glass of gorgeous, sweet red juice made from a pomegranate and a half.

◆

Arak

LEBANESE ANISE LIQUEUR

In Douma, *arak* making is a popular and common annual event with the grape harvest. Made from grapes that are fermented and flavored with anise seed, this highly prized liquor is served with dinner in tiny glasses. Sometimes diluted with water, it is transformed from a clear, water-like liquid to a milky opaque one.

Herbs, Spices & Fragrant Waters

Lebanese herbs, spices, fragrant waters and special ingredients can be purchased in Middle East food stores. There are many other ingredients and herbs not included in this list. See glossary section for more ingredients and tools.

HERBS

•*bebo'nage* – camomile, used for tea

•*ba'doonis* – parsley, flat-leaved, Italian parsley, rather than the curly variety more commonly used here; used in salads and as a garnish

•*baqleh barre, jewah* – purslane, wild or cultivated, used in salads, *fattoush, salata*, with *zeit, toum, limon*

•*basal akhdar* – green onions used in salads, stuffings, garnish and *mezza*

•*habak* - basil

•*kizbra* – cilantro, used with okra

•*na'na'* – mint, spearmint specifically; used fresh in salads, spinach pies, cabbage rolls or dried for use in *laban ou khyar*, cabbage rolls, *fattoush*, and other salads. Fresh leaves steeped for tea; good for stomach. Be sure to use spearmint rather than any of the other mints such as peppermint or bergamot which have such distinctly different flavors.

• *shimrah*– fresh fennel leaf used as flavoring in teas, also cooked with fava beans

'utar – scented geranium leaf used as flavoring in some desserts and preserves

warit ilgar – bay leaves, used in soups, broths

zaa'tar – an herb and the name of an herbal mixture of thyme, savory, sumac and sesame seeds. Mother says *zaa'tar* was called "the brain food" in Douma, because it was deemed to be so healthy to eat. There is an Arabic saying, "Bread and thyme opens the mind", undoubtedly referring to *tilmeh b'zaa'tar*. This mixture is used on baked bread, *tilmeh b'zaa'tar,* and is eaten mixed with olive oil and bread, cheese and olives

SPICES

bhar – allspice, whole or ground; used with lamb, chicken, *lubiyeh*

crawee – caraway seed, whole; used in bread baking, *kmege*

flefle – cayenne or black pepper; whole black peppers were ground; basic seasoning used in most savory dishes and salads; red cayenne available in mild, hot and super hot; we use red cayenne in most of our dishes

hab il'hal – cardamom pods, used in making Arabic coffee

irfe – cinnamon, whole or ground; sticks are used in lamb and chicken dishes; ground in mortar and pestle, sifted; enhances taste of the meat; cinnamon sticks also boiled to make tea, *chai l'irfe*

krimful – cloves, whole; used with stuffing chicken, lamb shanks, making lamb stock

mahlab – Cornell cherry kernels; used whole or ground in various pastry doughs for flavoring; *kurban,* cookies, *mamool*

mileh – salt; in the old country came in a cone and was ground; used as a preservative and for flavor

miski – mastic resin; ground with sugar for preserves in figs, quince, and in *booza*

sahlab – a powder extracted from an *orchis* plant root, salep; used in

making *booza* or mixed with warm milk and sprinkled with cinnamon as a beverage.

• *shimrah*- dried fennel seeds; used for making tea, also seasoning in cooking

•*summaq* - sumac; crushed deep red berries from the sumac tree used as spice; tart in flavor from malic acid in the berries so it is used when lemon is unavailable as a substitute in *fattoush, tabbouli*, grape leaves, *malfouf*

•*yensoon* - anise seed; ground for pastry doughs, whole in *ammah*; in making *arak* and tea

FRAGRANT WATERS

◆

•*attar* - simple syrup flavored with *may warid* or *may zahar,* used on pastries

•*may warid* - rose water, used to flavor pastries, tea, soft drinks, and lemonade

•*may zahar* - orange and lemon flower water; used to flavor pastries and syrups for pastries, with nuts, in dough batter; stimulant, sprinkled in home on special occasions to eliminate odors; stored air tight in a bottle kept in the dark.

• *'utar* - scented geranium flower water or a scented geranium leaf used in making some desserts and fruit preserves

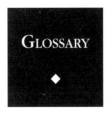

GLOSSARY

◆

Abouna	Father; priest
akkidinne	loquat trees and fruit
burghul	bulgar; wheat that is boiled and then cracked (different from cracked wheat which is not boiled); a range of sizes from small to large are used depending on the dish; smaller sizes are used in salads, *tabbouli* or *safsouf*; coarser sizes are used in cooked dishes.
citric acid	derived from citric fruits, similar in appearance to salt, and used as a lemon substitute in our cooking; available from wine-making suppliers or Middle East import stores
Douma	town in northern Lebanon's Batroun region
fistook	pistachio nuts
ghadda	lunch; the main meal of the day
halaweh	sesame seed confection eaten with bread for dessert (halva)
hesroum	sour green grapes mashed and strained, the liquid used in *hommous* and *baba ghannouj* as a lemon substitute
khoobz	Arabic bread
Jiddo	grandfather
jibn	soft, unripened Neufchatel-type cheese
kishk	dried yogurt and bulgar ground into a coarse flour
kousa abiad	light green Lebanese squash
laban	yogurt
labne	yogurt cheese; salted yogurt, drained in cheesecloth
limon	lemon
mezza	hors d'oeuvres
roube	yogurt starter
samne m'fatse	clarified butter
Sitto	grandmother

ALICE'S KITCHEN
GLOSSARY & MISCELLANEA

tabbouli	salad
tahini	sesame seed butter
teen	fig trees and fruit
Um	mother
warak 'inab	grape leaves
zibde	butter
zoom	sauce, usually tomato, from a stew

TOOLS
◆

hawin	mortar and pestle
ibree'	water pitcher used in Lebanon
matahne	grinder for coffee, pepper, allspice and other spices
manara	corer for *kousa* and eggplant
malat	pincer for cookies
qalb	*falafel* ejecting tool
toule	cutting board
sikkine	knife
mabrad	sharpener
raqwi	Arabic coffee pot
shoubak	rolling pin

ARABIC FOOD RELATED EXPRESSIONS
◆

Ahlan Wa Sahlan	Welcome to our home
Inshallah	God willing
Mabrouk!	Congratulations!
Sahteyn	Double health, bon apetite!
Sallem dayetkoom	God bless your hands, said to the cook as a complement for an excellent meal
T'faddalou	Welcome to the table, dinner is served

ALICE'S KITCHEN
GLOSSARY & MISCELLANEA

Sample Menus
◆

◆**Meals**

In Lebanon, there are three meals a day with the main meal at 1 or 2, followed by a siesta. Typically there is a very light breakfast and dinner. Bread, cheese, olives, fresh vegetables, *labne, halaweh* were served with every meal and might serve as breakfast or dinner.

◆*Terwea*

Breakfast is usually light—fresh fruits, fruit juice, fresh-squeezed orange juice, eggs in a variety of styles, *ijhee, labne, laban*, cheese, olives, honey, Arabic bread, *dibbis* (grape molasses), fig and other jams, *zaa'tar* with *zeit, tilme b'zaa'tar, tilme b' kishk, ammah* (winter wheat hot cereal), *halaweh jazariyeh* made with carrots and pumpkin, *jlunt*, coffee, tea; special breakfasts of Lebanese nut or cheese-filled sweetened crepes, *atayif b'louz* or *jibn*.

◆*Ghadda*

Lunch or main meal of the day in Lebanon—always served with bread, cheese, olives, fresh vegetables. Seasonal cooking is typical to our cuisine—buying what is in season, fresh and not too expensive; for example: fresh bean dishes in spring, summer; dried beans in fall, winter. Chard and spinach in fall, winter and spring; cucumbers, summer squash, tomato salads, *tabbouli* in summer. Following are a few combinations of what might be included in a well-balanced meal.

•*m'jaddrah, hommous*, fried eggplant, *salata*
•*laham mishwi, salata*
•*malfouf mihshi, waraq 'inab, salata*
•*tabbouli* served on a bed of romaine lettuce, *baba ghannouj*
•lentil soup, *fattoush*, fried eggplant or *kousa*
•*kousa mihshi*, cut vegetables, cheese, olives
•*tabbouli, kousa mihshi, sheikh al mihshi, sfeeha, tilme b'zaa'tar*
•*djej ou sh'ariyeh,* carrots, cucumbers
•*riz ou fassoulia* or *loubiyeh*, cut vegetables, *hommous*
•*kibbe bil sineyeh*, cucumber yogurt salad, *loubiyeh b'zeit*

◆*MEZZA*—SEE *MEZZA* CHAPTER FOR SUGGESTIONS

◆*ASHA*
Dinner—In Lebanon, a healthful custom is to have a very light dinner—usually a little bread, cheese, vegetables, and olives with some fruit. In the United States, we tend to have our largest meal at dinner. See *ghadda,* above, for additional meal ideas.

•*riz ou kousa,* carrots, cucumbers, bread, cheese, olives
•*waraq 'inab, laban ou khyar,* bread, cheese, olives
•lentil soup, *salata,* bread, cheese, olives

◆DESSERTS
Fresh seasonal fruit is our traditional dessert served after meals. Grapes, figs, apples, pears, oranges, apricots, plums, peaches, persimmons, pomegranates, bananas, pineapples, watermelons, canteloupes, loquats, basically whatever is available and in season. In winter—*halaweh* (halva) with bread or dried fruits, or jams such as fig, *sfargel,* quince jam. Later in the evening, hot *ammah* is a winter treat, as is *zlebiyeh. Riz ib haleeb,* rice pudding, is refreshing in warm weather. Cookies or pastries were served with coffee or tea to guests in the afternoon or evening, not usually as dessert.

FOODS AND HOLIDAYS

•*Ammah*—sweetened, boiled wheat berries served with nuts and raisins; a less brothy version of *ammah* was made by families when there was a death; this was traditionally served at church in little paper cups at the memorial service. Also it was served to celebrate births.

•*Kurban*—host communion, offering for the dead, Easter, Christmas.

•Cookies—were made at holiday times, *baklawa* at Christmas, Easter *mamool*

•Weddings—*mamool, graibee, sfeeha, kibbe*

•New Year's Day—*ammah, zlebiyeh*

•St. Barbara, Halloween—*ammah* served with pine nuts, walnuts, pistachio nuts, raisins; *awamette,* Lebanese doughnuts; lentil sprouts

A typical Doumani Garden *JNEYNE*

◆

◆**Vegetables**

Romaine lettuce, bell pepper, tomato, green onion, okra, eggplant, *batinjan arabi* (similar to Japanese), cucumber, *miiti*, Armenian cucumber, *kousa*, cabbage.

◆**Herbs**

Lebanese parsley, *baa'doonis*—a flat-leafed parsley; one plant was left to go to seed, to be collected and sown for a new patch.

Mint, *na'na*, dies back in winter; perennial; propagated from root cuttings.

Garlic, *toum,* is used raw primarily, mashed into a paste for dressings and sauces, but sometimes used in cooked dishes.

◆**Flowers**

zahra : cosmos, marigolds, tulips, daffodils, narcissus, roses—many of the same flowers we have in North America

◆**Lebanese fruits and nuts grown or enjoyed in Douma**

almond-*louz*, apricot, apple, quince, pear, plum, peach, orange, banana, cherry-*caraz,* fig-*teen*, lemon-*limon hammid*, sweet lemon-*limon hillou*, olive-*zeitune*, loquat-*akkidinne,* pomegranate-*rimman;* persimmon-*qaqi,* walnut-*jouz;* filbert, *arishe*-grape arbors abound

THE ELIAS SAWAYA DINNER PARTY

Mrs. Dalal Ganamey, Mr. & Mrs. Elias Sawaya & daughters & Mr. & Mrs. Edmond Ganamey.

Salaam alaikum!
Sahteyn ou Y'slamou Hal Eidine!

Alice's Kitchen
Glossary & Miscellanea

Index

ALICE'S KITCHEN
INDEX

ALICE'S KITCHEN
INDEX

Our tradition is about living gently on the earth. Using resources of the earth respectfully. Sharing and preparing food with love. Eating what is in season. Growing our own food as much as possible. Living simply and richly. Honoring the earth. Honoring ourselves and each other. This is my gesture to honor and preserve that culture for myself, for my family and for others who appreciate these traditions, values and foods. My love for our food and culture continues to grow.

A portion of the proceeds of the sales of **Alice's Kitchen** will benefit the people of Lebanon. Thank you for joining us in **Alice's Kitchen**.

♥

ABOUT THE AUTHOR

◆

Linda **Dalal Sawaya** is a cook, painter, children's book illustrator, photographer, graphic designer, and writer. As the youngest of five daughters of Lebanese immigrants, Alice and Elias, she was born and raised in Los Angeles, and grew up in Alice's kitchen—where cooking became one of her passions, along with baking bread and gardening. As a young child, she shared a bed with her grandmother, namesake, and inspiration, Dalal, who also graced and blessed Alice's kitchen with her skill and loving presence.

Sawaya received a Bachelor of Arts design degree from UCLA where she found a passion for photography. During a time living in the splendid Santa Cruz mountains of California, she photographed children creating natural, black and white environmental portraits.

Having been a culinary artist in professional settings, of both Lebanese and vegetarian cuisines in California and Oregon, Sawaya prefers the venue of preparing meals and baking for family and friends in her own cozy kitchen. Writing and editing has been a part of her career since her 1977 move to Oregon and has continued as a natural outgrowth of working as publication and graphic designer.

In 1986 she started painting and fell in love with it. Integrating media—photography, painting, ceramics—she is currently using photography in her painting and is painting on clay. Her work has been exhibited in galleries in Oregon, Los Angeles, New York and Santa Cruz. Sawaya's work has been published on the covers of numerous books which she has illustrated and designed: including *Food For Our Grandmothers: Writings by Arab-American Feminists, My Grandmother's Cactus, Khalil Gibran: His Life and World.*

One of Sawaya's paintings, published in the *Aramco World* article, "Memories of a Lebanese Garden" (Jan/Feb 1997) that was excerpted from *Alice's Kitchen*, is included in a new anthology by

Naomi Shihab Nye, poet and writer extraordinaire, *The Space Between Our Footsteps: Poems and Paintings from the Middle East.*

Linda has illustrated two children's books, both published in 1995. The first, *How to Get Famous in Brooklyn*, was selected as one of the best children's books of the year for exhibition in New York by The New York Society of Illustrators. *The Little Ant/La Hormiga Chiquita*, a delightful bilingual Mexican folk tale, was selected as one of The Bank Street Best Children's Books of the Year. Illustrating and writing children's books, working with children in schools are joyful and passionate parts of her life.

Last year Sawaya traveled to Lebanon, with a greatly appreciated grant from the Regional Arts & Culture Council that allowed her to return for the first time in twenty-five years, to research a variety of book and art projects. The trip was joyous and stimulating—this edition of **Alice's Kitchen** includes a few photographs from that trip, not to mention recipes and inspiration. The love experienced reuniting with family and homeland after so many years was a cherished gift that continues to fill her heart.

Children's Books illustrated by Linda Dalal Sawaya

■ *The Little Ant/La Hormiga Chiquita* published by Rizzoli International, written by Michael Rose Ramirez, September 1995, ISBN 0-8478-1922-1

■ *How to Get Famous in Brooklyn*, published by Simon and Schuster Books for Young Readers, written by Amy Hest, September 1995, ISBN 0-689-80293-5

About Alice

❤

Alice **Ganamey Sawaya**, an epicurian Lebanese immigrant, is a mother of five, grandmother of seven, greatgrandmother of five, an artist, octogenarian, and inspiration to all. Her story, and that of her mother, Dalal, are found in the introduction of **Alice's Kitchen**.